Walks from Your

Windermere and Kendal

by
Tom Bowker & Mick North

Dalesman Books
1991

The Dalesman Publishing Company Ltd.,
Clapham, via Lancaster, LA2 8EB

First published 1984
Third edition 1991

ISBN: 1 85568 016 5

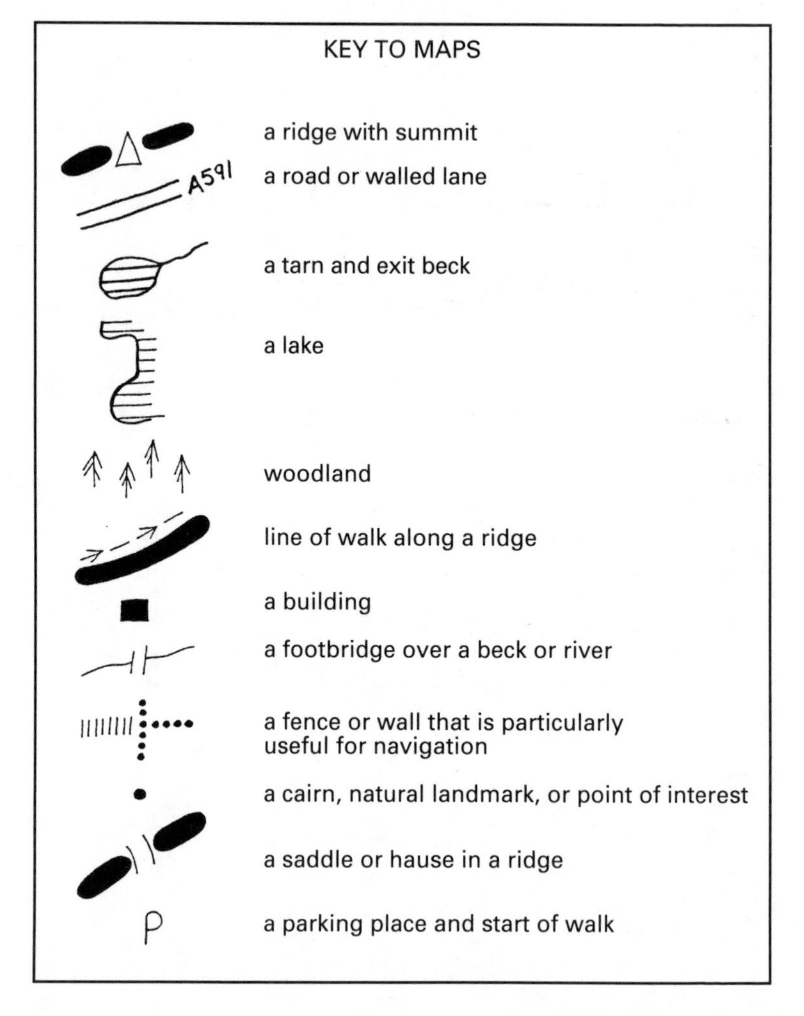

Printed by Peter Fretwell & Sons Ltd., Keighley, England.

Contents

Page

INTRODUCTION 4

WINDERMERE

Walk 1. John Bell's Banner and Woundale 6
Walk 2. Froswick, Ill Bell and Yoke by the Roman Road . 8
Walk 3. Sour Hows, Garburn Pass and Kentmere Hall ... 10
Walk 4. Claife Heights and the Lake Shore 12
Walk 5. Orrest Head and Brant Fell 14
Walk 6. Windermere's South-Western Shore 17
Walk 7. Gummer's How and St. Anthony's Chapel 20

STAVELEY

Walk 8. The Upper Kentmere Valley 23
Walk 9. Potter Tarn, Gurnal Dubhs and the Kent Valley . 25

KENDAL

Walk 10. Harter Fell from Long Sleddale 29
Walk 11. Keld, Swindale and Shap Abbey 31
Walk 12. The Whinfell Ridge and Borrowdale 35
Walk 13. A Circuit of Skeggles Water 38
Walk 14. Scout Scar and Cunswick Fell 40
Walk 15. Levens Park, the River Kent, and the old
Lancaster Canal 44
Walk 16. Whitbarrow Scar 46

Cover design by Susan Smith.

Introduction

THIS guidebook is not for the motorist who is looking for a couple of miles' stroll in driving shoes. Nor is it for the hardened long-distance fellwalker. It is written principally for the motorist-cum-walker who is prepared to pull on a pair of boots or stout walking shoes, sling a small pack on his back and be happy to be out for at least two to three hours. Many of the walks described may also appeal to family parties; to those introducing their children to the hills. For there are many facets to these walks other than the attaining of summits. There are tarns and pools for bathing, woods, waterfalls, lovely picnic spots and caves that would appeal to children. All the walks are circular, starting and finishing at the same point but returning by a different route to that embarked upon in order to add interest. The walks described are divided into three types.

1. **Valley Walks.** There are only two genuine circular valley walks in this booklet for the simple reason that they are hard to find. The two main problems are that the nearer to valley level the more problems with access across private and farm land, and that the very nature of Lakeland tends to force the walker uphill eventually. The two described however are good of their type and certainly worth exploring. We generally advise boots or stout walking shoes but given dry conditions the training-type shoe would be perfectly adequate for these walks. It must be remembered however that any Lakeland walk will have its boggy patches and that care must be taken on wet or slimy rocks at the edges of becks, rivers and waterfalls.

2. **Medium Walks.** These are walks that range over summits below the two-thousand feet level. They form the bulk of the walks in the booklet for we felt they would appeal most to the kind of motorist-cum-walker-cum-family party described above. They do however cover similar type of ground to the fell-walks of Section 3 and strictly speaking the same rules about clothing and footwear described in that section apply here. Given dry summer conditions however some of these walks could be done in lighter footgear but care must be taken.

3. **Fell Walks.** These are walks that reach one or more summits over two thousand feet above sea level. They are not however strenuous walks of their type, either being of no great length or over relatively easy ground. Where there is any possibility of the walker getting into difficulty easier alternatives are given. Nevertheless these are fell-walks and should be treated with respect, especially in bad or winter conditions. We do not wish to labour the point but would not rest easy if we did not enumerate here a few basic rules. It is advisable

to wear boots, carry a map, compass, whistle and waterproofs. In winter conditions a torch, gloves, balaclava, spare sweater, a plastic survival bag and spare food are advisable additions. Loose fitting jeans are okay in summer but warmer covering is advisable in winter. Never be afraid to turn back if the weather deteriorates and if you are forced to use your compass start using it at a point where you know where you are, then you have a fixed point to return to — don't wait until you are lost.

All the walks described are accompanied by a rough sketch-map. In clear weather, used sensibly and combined with the text, they should be more than adequate. It is advised however, particularly for the fell-walks, to also carry the one-inch Ordnance Survey 'Tourist' Map, or the applicable sheet of the Ordnance Survey, 'The English Lakes' 1:25000 Outdoor Leisure Maps. As well as being a better aid to navigation, the Leisure Maps being particularly highly detailed, they also, especially the one-inch, help you identify the various lakes and peaks seen from a particular summit or viewpoint. The mileages are approximate and 'left' or 'right' refers to an object as facing it. The parking facilities described are as at the moment of writing. Local authorities often proscribe certain areas and open up others so please don't blame the authors if a particular parking situation differs from the description, it is as accurate and up-to-date as the authors can make it.

All the walks described here are on official rights-of-way; or permissive footpaths; or on public access areas. Routes can however be legally changed from time to time by developments or road improvements, in which case there should be a signpost specifically indicating the alteration. Readers of the previous booklets in this series may notice a lack of detailed views in this particular one. This is because whilst researching it we were almost constantly plagued by low cloud and rain.

Our interest in the past has always been with the high fells. As the work progressed however we found ourselves becoming fascinated by hills and footpaths that we must admit we had previously ignored. We only hope that the readers of this booklet discover as much pleasure from these walks as we did. Happy walking!

Tom Bowker and Mick North

WINDERMERE

Walk 1 **Fell Walk, 4 miles**

John Bell's Banner and Woundale

This is one of the easiest and safest ways of reaching the summit of a Lakeland two-thousand five-hundred footer. You are nearly fifteen-hundred feet above sea level when you leave your car on Kirkstone Pass and the path climbs alongside a wall virtually all the way from the back door of the inn to the summit cairn. The advantage of having a high start results in the walk lacking variation but you can't have it both ways; a return via Woundale does compensate for this to some extent.

Parking: Opposite the Kirkstone Pass Inn *on the summit of Kirkstone Pass (GR 402081).*

RED SCREES, the rugged mountain facing the inn, is a more exhilarating climb than John Bell's Banner. The line is obvious, a natural fault slanting from left to right up the steep craggy face. An easier alternative lies around to the left in the corrie that so obviously gives the mountain its name. Red Screes however falls within the boundaries of a companion volume (*Walks From Your Car: Ambleside and Grasmere*) and a longer and more varied route up it is described in that booklet.

For John Bell's Banner follow the well-worn path, starting to the left of the inn, that climbs up to a gap in a wall where it turns right to follow that wall to reach a large cairn on the crest of St. Raven's Edge. Turn left here and follow the path, alongside a wall, along the undulating crest of the ridge before dropping into a dip. Beyond the wall on your right here is Woundale and this dip is the point on your return where you will branch off. For the ascent continue with the path alongside the wall which begins to climb again all the time bearing to the right. When the wall veers even more sharply to the right a cairn surmounted by a cross will be seen crowning the skyline to your left. This is a memorial to one Mark Atkinson, a licensee of the *Kirkstone Pass Inn* for many years, and from it there is a fine view of Kirkstone Pass. The wall continues across the grassy plateau, passing to the right of a small tarn, to reach the junction of walls that is the summit. There are several cairns about, all of which seem higher than the one you are standing by. To the north-west there is a distant

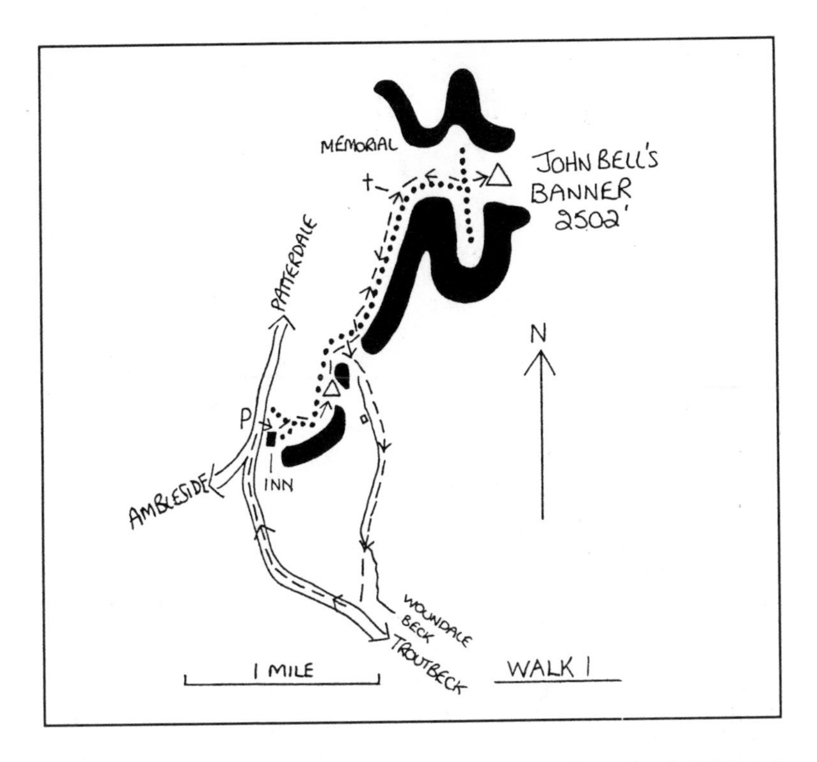

but comprehensive view of the rugged eastern flanks of Fairfield and Helvellyn. To the east, across the gulf of Thresthwaite Mouth, the graceful summit cairn of Thornthwaite Crag beckons, with the dome of High Street to its left. Froswick and Ill Bell (Walk 2) look their shapely best to the south-east and below them the green hollow of Troutbeck leads the eye down to gleaming Windermere. It's worth wandering to the north-western and north-eastern rims for the 'bird's-eye' views down into Caudale and Threshthwaite Cove.

Return by the same route until you reach the dip below St. Raven's Edge. Go through a gap in the wall to your left and follow the beck downhill. There is no distinct path until after a large sheep-fold is passed then tractor tracks will be seen on the left-hand bank. The Woundale Beck is pleasantly cascaded in its lower reaches. Just before the ground levels out a ruin will be passed, on your right. Once the valley floor is reached the path becomes wider and firmer and runs alongside a wall. Near the valley mouth the beck, which swings left preparatory to plunging into the Troutbeck Valley, is crossed by a slabby footbridge. Soon a gate and stile leads onto the A592. Turn right and follow it back up to Kirkstone Pass.

Walk 2 **Fell Walk, 8 miles**

Froswick, Ill Bell and Yoke by the Roman Road

A fairly energetic fell walk but on well-worn paths all the way. Even in mist the ridge is well-defined and the route obvious. The path up the valley can be boggy in wet conditions. The remaining traces of the Roman Road appear as just another fell path but it must be a dull soul whose imagination is not stirred when toiling up its steep zig-zags. The views from the ridge are very fine, especially to the west and south.

Parking: From the south the A592 Windermere to Penrith road crosses a bridge over the Trout Beck before passing between Troutbeck Church and School. Park either in a lay-by just beyond the church or down a side road just beyond the bridge, on the banks of the beck (GR 414028).

WALK UP the A592 to reach the entrance of Limefitt Camping and Caravan Site, where a 'Public Bridleway' sign will be seen. Follow the road down through the camp and up towards the farm. Just before reaching the farm turn left (◀ Television Lounge) in front of camp ablutions and 'Scullery'. Beyond them bear right through a gap in a wall onto a stony track which heads towards the rear of the farm. Turn left, around a wall, to reach an iron gate. Go through the gate and follow the path keeping a wall to your left.

Continue with this path for about three-quarters of a mile to reach and pass to the right of Long Green Head Farm. Beyond the farm pass through a gate and continue, with a wall to your left. Ahead, to your right, are the shapely summits of Yoke, Ill Bell and Froswick, your objectives. The bulkier peak beyond them, at the head of the valley, is Thornthwaite Crag; you may be able to pick out the Roman road zig-zagging up its lower slopes. The lower but dominant peak in the centre of the valley is The Tongue. Traces of an Ancient British settlement have been found on its crest. The craggy fell rising behind and to the left of The Tongue is John Bell's Banner (Walk 1). Across the valley to your left rises Wansfell with the A592 slanting across its flanks and up towards Kirkstone Pass.

The path eventually bears away from the wall and after crossing a stream passes to the right of a barn. Continue ahead, with a wall to your left, into the narrow valley between The Tongue and the Ill Bell range. Eventually the wall veers away. Continue, with a beck (Hagg Gill) below and to your left, towards some obvious quarry spoil heaps, with a barn beyond. The path passes below the spoil heaps then bears left across a bridge over the gill, below the barn, and up to a gate. The gate leads onto another track, turn right along this.

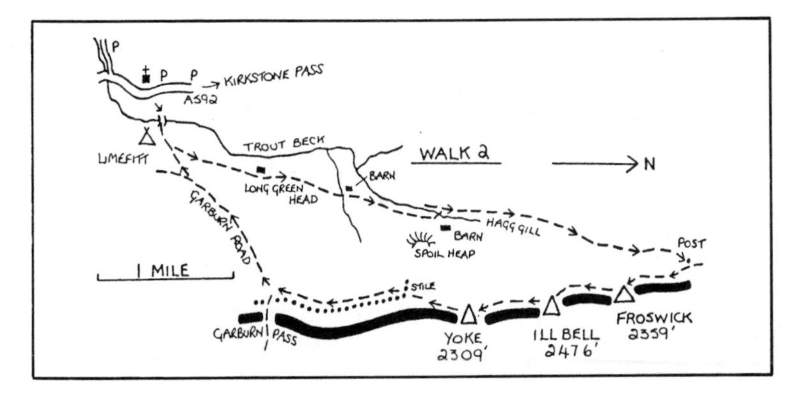

When the right-hand wall turns away the track divides. Ignore the left-hand track heading up the fellside and drop down and across a flattish area. The zig-zags of the Roman road can be clearly seen ahead climbing up to the left of a steep gill. After crossing the flattish area follow the path up to a gate in a wall. Beyond this the path steepens, with a wall to the left and gill to its right. The wall eventually veers away to the left but you continue up the obvious path which starts to zig-zag up the fellside. The broader zig-zags are the remnants of the road connecting the Roman forts at Penrith and Ambleside, traditionally known as the High Street, a name now usually given to the fell that forms the highest point of the road.

The path eventually reaches the crest of the ridge below and to the right of an old iron fence stanchion. The far side of the ridge drops abruptly down into the Kentmere valley and below is Kentmere Reservoir (Walk 8). The fells forming the far side of the valley are the Harter Fell — Kentmere Pike ridge (Walk 10). Turn right and follow the worn path down the ridge into a dip before climbing up to the summit of Froswick. Another dip and a steeper climb leads to the rockier summit of Ill Bell and its trio of fine cairns. Beyond Ill Bell the ridge drops steeply again before rising and levelling out into the flattish summit of Yoke. From all points on this fine trio of peaks there is an extensive view to the south towards Windermere and the wooded hills of Furness and south-west and west to the Coniston and Central Fells.

From the summit of Yoke the path leads down the ridge to a stile over a wall. Cross this and keeping the wall to your left continue down to meet the track crossing over the ridge at the crest of Garburn Pass. Turn right here and follow this track, eventually between walls, down towards Troutbeck. Eventually a large plantation, overgrowing old quarry workings, will be met on your left. Whilst passing this look for a small foot-stile over the fence on your right, just beyond where a wall climbs up from the valley. Cross this and follow the steep path downhill to rejoin your outgoing path behind Limefitt camp site.

Sour Hows, Garburn Pass and Kentmere Hall

A walk giving a variety of all-round views that is nowhere really strenuous despite its length. The hardest section is the climb up Sour Hows and that can be avoided by a slightly less energetic variation. Kentmere Hall is a fine example of a 'pele' tower and a reminder that these now peaceful valleys and fells may have once been the scene of raiding and burning. The latter half of the walk can be a bit boggy in wet weather.

Parking: From Windermere take the A591 towards Kendal. Approximately two miles along this road, just before reaching the hamlet of Ings, look out for a side turning to the left signposted 'Troutbeck'. Follow this road until you reach the entrance to the second road on your right, the one after the one signposted 'High Borrans'. Park hereabouts (GR 424006).

FOLLOW this rough road eventually passing to the right of Dubhs Reservoir. Ahead you will see Red Screes rising beyond the ridge of Wansfell. To your left, beyond the reservoir and through the trees, a glimpse of the Coniston Fells can be had. Soon the left-hand slope falls away giving a view down into the Troutbeck Valley with the village straggling along its opposite wall. To the left a glimpse of Windermere will be seen with the Coniston and Langdale Fells beyond. The road swings to the right and ahead, beyond a plantation, there is a fine view of the fells around the valley head. The skyline reads, from left to right, Red Screes, John Bell's Banner (Walk 1), followed by the dip of Threshthwaite Mouth, with the prominent shape of The Tongue below it, followed by the shapely trio of Froswick, Ill Bell and Yoke (Walk 2).

As you approach the plantation look for stiles over the walls to your left and right. For those who desire to take in the summit of Sour Hows, climb over the stile to your right. A slightly less energetic variation is to continue along the track, passing above the plantation, to a junction with the Garburn Pass track; turn right here to reach the crest of the pass. For the more energetic, after crossing the stile climb steeply uphill following a faint path which bears left towards where rocky ribs thrust from the fellside. The faint path follows these ribs to reach a wooden stile over a wall. Beyond this the angle eases and the summit of Sour Hows is reached. There are several grassy hummocks, all of which seem of identical height, although one is crowned by a miniscule cairn.

Look north to see a wall undulating across the fell. Head towards it

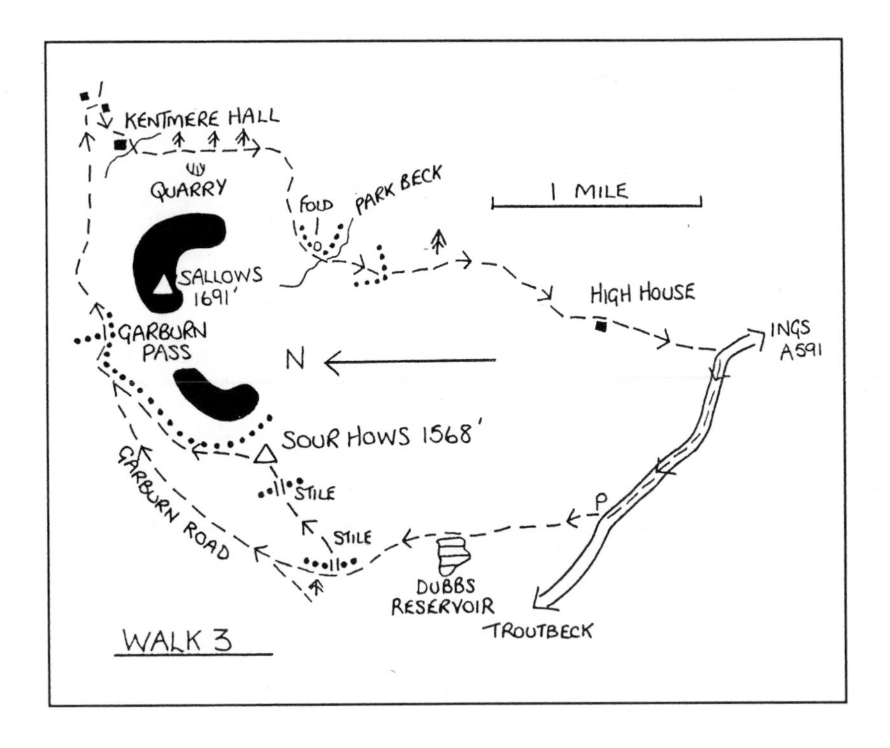

and follow it to reach the crest of Garburn Pass and a junction with the easier variation. Turn right along the well-worn track to pass through a gate. You are now on one of Lakeland's ancient highways. Scots raiders (by repute), pedlars, cattle-drovers and pack ponies bearing slate, timber, charcoal, salt, etc., have all passed this way. Beyond the gate the path twists down towards Kentmere village. As you descend the tower of Kentmere Hall will be seen over the wall to your right.

The path eventually drops between walls to meet a tarmac road. Look for a sign on the building on your right indicating 'Kentmere Hall' that way. Pass between farm buildings, through a gate, and follow a path towards a barn with a white footpath marker on its left-hand corner. Pass to the left of the barn through a gap in a wall and slant leftwards across the field to an iron gate marked 'Footpath'. Pass through this and head to the right down the field towards Kentmere Hall. Pass to the left of a hen hut and go down to a gate. Go through this and turn immediately left through another gate. At the end of the building turn right and head across a concrete apron to a gate marked with blue arrow and sign 'Bridleway'. Look to your right here for a fine view of the decrepit tower of Kentmere Hall. It was the ancestral home of the Gilpins, a talented Cumbrian family who named medieval warriors, Reformation preachers, Elizabethan diplomats and eighteenth century educational reformers among their number.

Cross the stream by a concrete bridge and follow the obvious track heading uphill to the left. Soon an old quarry will be seen on your right. Eventually the angle eases and the wall to the right veers away. Continue, keeping the wall to your left and ignoring a tractor track veering off to your right. Eventually you will reach a gate, just beyond a sheepfold to your left, which leads onto the bank of a beck — Park Beck. Turn left, downstream, until shortly you will see a subsidiary beck joining on the far side. Cross the main beck and follow this branching beck up a small ravine containing a solitary tree to reach a fenced gap in a wall. Turn left here and follow the wall to reach a gate in a corner. Go through this and follow a path, with a wall to your left, beyond which is a plantation surrounded by a wall.

Continue with wall to your left to a gate leading into a walled lane. Follow the lane. Eventually the left wall veers away. Continue with wall to your right all the time bearing right to a gate in a corner. Pass through this and continue with wall to your right to a further gate leading into a walled lane. Go through this and turn immediately right through a gate. Follow a green path which swings left to a gate in a wall near a tree. Pass through this and keeping wall on your left climb between banks then down to a gate in a corner near another tree. Pass through this gate and continue across the field, bearing left into a walled lane which leads down to High House Farm. Go through the farmyard and turn left onto the farm road. Follow this tarmac strip down to the Ings-Troutbeck road. Turn right along this in order to reach your car.

Walk 4 **Medium Walk, 4½ miles**

Claife Heights and the Lakeshore

A pleasant walk, although occasionally boggy, with virtually all the climbing done in the first mile. There is more open ground than you would expect and the variety of views is splendid. The stretch along the lakeshore is a delightful finish.

Parking: Cross the ferry. After driving off the ferry keep your eyes open for a car-park in the woods on your right just around a rocky corner. Park here. Or, alternatively, park your car in Bowness and walk down to the ferry (GR 387954).

FOLLOW the footpath signposted 'Claife Heights' out of the right-hand side of the car-park. It soon climbs steeply up through the trees, below some greenish rocks, to reach an imposing ruined building overlooking the lake and ferry. This is the ruin of a 'viewing station'. During the first great wave of Lakeland tourism in the nineteenth century it wasn't enough just to visit Lakeland and see its beauties; it had to be done in the fashionable manner from specially constructed 'stations'. This particular one belonged to the now defunct Ferry Hotel and the windows were glazed with coloured glass to give an added effect.

Pass under the arch and follow the path between rocks and then uphill, following faded white footpath indicators. The path zig-zags steeply before the angle eases and a fence is met with a plantation beyond. Turn right here and follow the obvious path. There is a fine view to the right down onto Belle Island and Bowness Bay. Further up the lake the Troutbeck valley can be seen cutting deeply into the fells. The path goes between a fence and a wall and eventually meets a kissing-gate leading onto a lane signposted ◀ 'Hawkshead/Lake Shore' ▶. Turn left. Eventually a walled lane, heading up to the right, will be met signposted 'Hawkshead' that way. Turn right up the lane. Behind you as you climb is a glimpse of Windermere with Gummers How (Walk 7) rising beyond it, and perhaps beyond that a distant view of the Pennines. Over the wall to your left is a glimpse of the Coniston Fells. (For the next mile you are covering the same ground as Walk 11, 'The Three Tarns and Claife Heights', in a companion volume to the Coniston and Hawkshead area).

Soon the left-hand wall veers away and the path turns right to follow the right-hand wall, passing to the right of a scummy pond. Eventually a gate is reached beyond which the path divides. Near the wall to your right should be a signpost indicating 'Hawkshead' straight ahead, in the direction of the wall. Continue this way downhill, eventually to go between a fence and wall. Soon a stile is crossed and ahead the path can be seen bearing steeply up to the left. As you climb up this look to your right for a glimpse of Windermere. When the ground levels off look for a path leading to the right through the trees and a gap in an old wall. Follow this out into the open onto a rocky ridge which gives a superb bird's-eye view down onto the island-studded waist of Windermere. The largest island is Belle Isle, the home of the Curwen family for many generations.

Return back to the original path and turn right to continue along it. Shortly a diversion of ways and a signpost indicating ◀ 'Hawkshead/Belle Grange' ▶ are met. Turn right and follow the path onto a flat rock crowned by a cairn. Pass this and go through a gap in a wall to where the path turns left. Follow this path which keeps close to

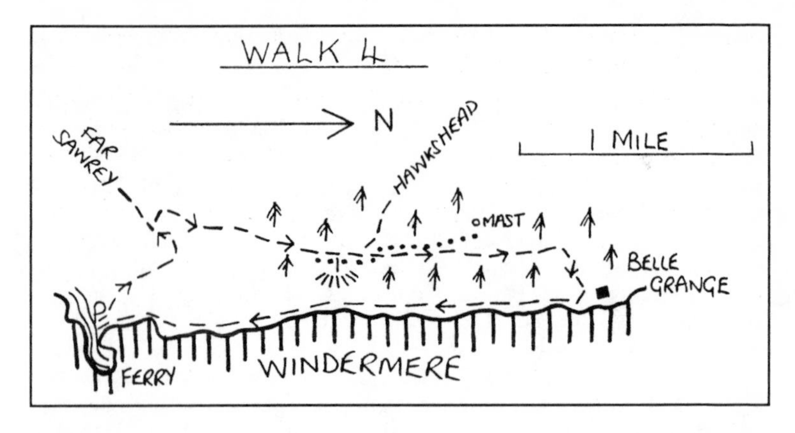

the wall at first then gradually bears away from it. There are views of Windermere to the right, with the head of the lake coming into view and the Fairfield Fells rising beyond it. The tower of a radio/television relay station will be seen rising above the trees to your left. The path eventually drops down to join a broader track signposted 'Bridleway'. Turn right along this. This track zig-zags down over once well-constructed steps to meet the garden wall of Belle Grange. Follow this wall down to meet a broader track. Turn right along this.

This track at first runs high above the lake but after passing over a cattlegrid eventually moves down to the lakeshore. Given the right conditions the walk can end with an impromptu lakeside picnic, sunbathe or dip. When the ferry road is reached turn right. To avoid following the road round the hazardous rocky corner look for a gap in the wall to your right at the first bend. A path leads from here to the car-park.

Walk 5 **Medium Walk, 4½ miles**

Orrest Head and Brant Fell

For a small expenditure of energy this short walk rewards you with superlative views that must be difficult to beat anywhere in Lakeland.

Parking: Park in the Lay-by on the A591 up the hill and to the right of the 'Windermere Hotel' (GR 415987).

FROM the lay-by, walk downhill past the front of the hotel. Continue past bus shelters to reach the start of a tarmac path signposted 'Orrest Head', on your right. Climb this path ignoring all side paths. The tarmac surface ends in front of a house. Continue up the path to a wooden clearing with an iron gate to its right. Ahead are three paths, take the central one tunnelling into the bushes. This path swings right upon approaching a wall and climbs up into a wall corner and then between a wall and fence. This narrower way leads to a kissing-gate on your left, beyond which a short climb leads on to the summit of Orrest Head and a superb all-round view. An indicator details the magnificent skyline which ranges from Coniston Old ,an, almost directly across Windermere, to the distant and flattish summit of Ingleborough away to the south-east.

Go past the indicator and follow a path down into a wall corner to find a stile. Cross this and head down and alongside a wall towards the right of Causeway Farm. A wall corner on your left is reached where a beck is spanned by a 'clapper' bridge. Do not cross the beck but turn right and follow it to shortly reach another 'clapper' bridge close to a wall corner on your right. Now turn right, away from the beck, keeping the wall on your left, to shortly reach a stile in a wall ahead marked by a yellow footpath indicator. Cross this stile and bear left across the field, keeping a wall on your left an ignoring a stile in it, to reach a further stile marked by a path indicator. Cross this and bear left again to round a wall corner and pass through a gate into a walled lane. Turn right and follow this lane to reach Common Farm. Go to the right of the farm buildings into a boggy lane sloping rightwards. Almost immediately look for a 'Public Footpath' sign on your left indicating up to a gate. Go through the gate and on to a tarmac road.

Turn right and follow this road to a junction with the A591 Kendal-Windermere road. Cross this to a stone and, beyond this, head rightwards across a field to join a path running alongside a wall. Turn left along this path. Ignore a stile soon seen crossing the wall to your right, but soon afterwards, when the path forks, take the right fork to reach a gate. Beyond this follow a path across a field to a gate with a wooden stile to its left. Go through the gate and follow a path to a railway crossing. As you cross there is an unusual view to your right of the Langdale Pikes rising above a gleaming curve of railway track.

Beyond the crossing a path leads into a housing estate. Turn left along the pavement. Soon you will see a path leading down to your left past a 'South Lakeland No Tipping' sign. This leads to a packhorse bridge spanning a beck. Cross this and turn right, following a 'School Knott' sign, to reach a gate. Beyond this the path climbs gently around the houses to eventually pass through a gate and to the right of a house before making a left turn. Almost immediately look for a 'Public

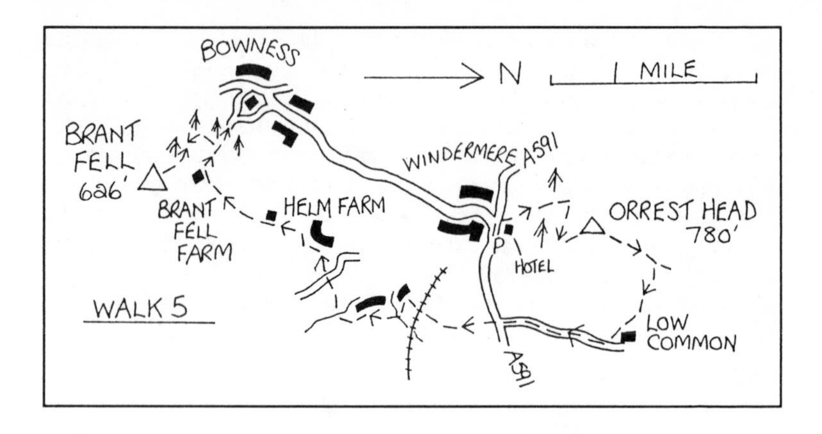

Footpath' sign which directs you right down stone steps, over a footbridge spanning a beck and over a stile into a field. Head up this field to a wall corner on your left. Go round this and follow the wall to a 'Public Footpath' sign and a stile leading on to a tarmac road.

Turn right, along the road, then almost immediately left through a signposted iron gate. There is a fine view of the head of Windermere and the fells beyond. Now follow a path down behind another housing estate. Cross a stile and zig-zag down to reach a three-armed signpost. Follow the central sign, pointing left. This path bears around the houses to a T-junction of paths. Turn left over a stile and follow a path to a gate and beyond to a stile leading on to a path near Helm Farm. Now head diagonally left to a white-painted stile in a wall. Beyond this, slant right across a field towards a wall corner. Brant Fell can be seen towering ahead now. Continue past the wall corner to reach a white-painted, and gated, wall stile. Beyond this follow a tarmac strip leftwards to a T-junction. Cross this and go across the grass to yet another paint marked wall stile. Cross this and the field beyond to a paint marked gate. Beyond this head, slightly leftwards, up a field to reach some double gates. Go through the iron gate and follow a path to shortly join a tarmac farm road near a cattle grid. DO NOT TURN LEFT UP THIS ROAD TO BRANT FELL FARM AS THIS IS A PRIVATE ROAD.

Cross the road and walk between walls to reach a double gate. Go through the metal gate and slant right down a field, alongside a wall, to a red metal gate leading onto a broader wooden path. Turn left and climb this path, passing several old stone benches to reach a gate. Go through the gate into a field and up on to a knoll giving a fine view down on to Windermere, with the Langdale Pikes rising prominently beyond. Now walk behind you to a wall corner and a handsome stone stile. Cross this and follow a path climbing rightwards through a stand of trees to emerge on to the open fellside. Head up to the obvious and fine cairn crowing the summit of Brant Fell and an extensive view of Windermere and its ring of delectable fells.

To return to your car either retrace your footsteps to the A591 and then turn left along it, or, continue down the 'stone bench' path past the red metal gate to join streets leading into Bowness. From Bowness walk up the main street back to Windermere.

Walk 6 **Medium Walk, 5 or 8 miles**

Windermere's South-Western Shore

Pleasant walking, mainly through a variety of woodland, but including a splendid stretch of lakeshore. The most expenditure of energy is during the first half mile, especially if the short version is done. The longer circuit requires a little more energy but offers a wider variety of scenery.

Parking: As for Walk 4.

GO BACK onto the road and turn right. Follow it uphill until you see Hawk Rigg Farm on your left. Just beyond the farm turn left at a footpath sign then almost immediately right into a narrow pathway. Follow this to a gate. Beyond this go down the field keeping the wall to your right. Near the foot of the field look for a gate in this wall. Beyond this bear left, across the corner of a field, to a further gate. Beyond this head downhill, with Town End church to your right, to a gate signposted 'Ferry Hill'.

Turn left along the road past cottages then turn almost immediately right through a gate signposted 'Footpath'. Cross a footbridge over a beck to a divergence of paths. Look for a small footpath sign ahead and to your left, with a banked path to its right. Follow this. The path curves around to the right, above a sloping field,

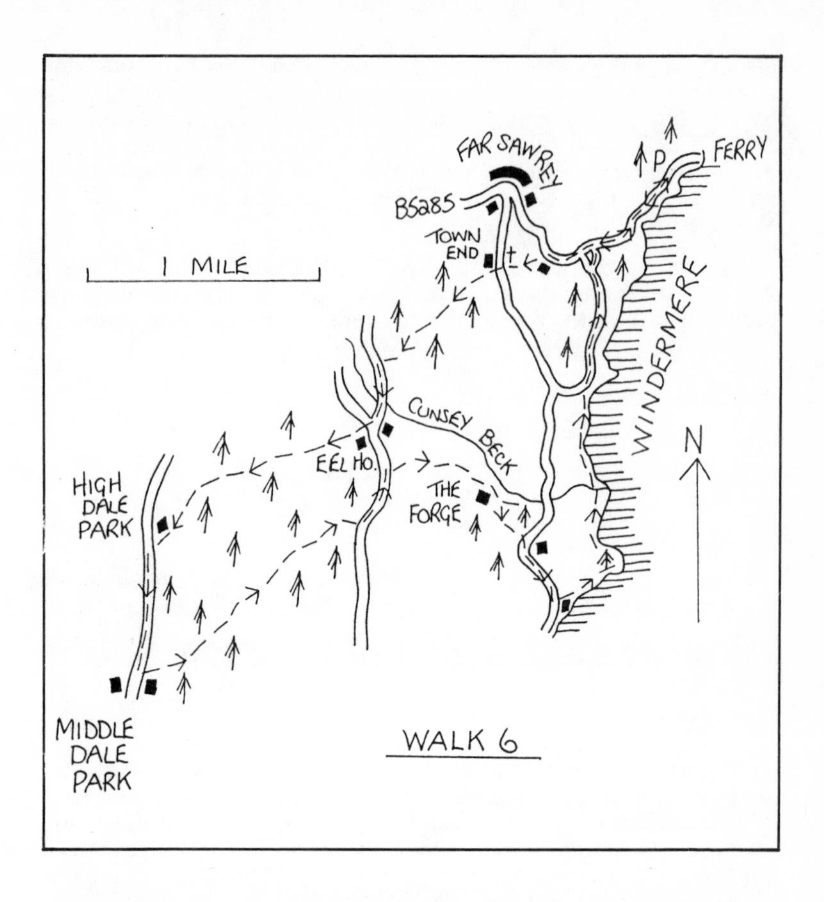

before swinging left to a stile. Cross the stile and continue with the path, which bears right between a fence and trees. The path leads through a gate then swings up to the left just before reaching a stile. Cross the stile and follow a path beyond which leads across a field enclosed on three sides by woods. At the end of the field cross a stile and follow the path down into a wood. Soon an old wall is crossed and a deer fence met to your left. Follow the path alongside the fence to cross a rutted forestry road. Continue with the path alongside the fence gradually descending until a tarmac road is seen, down to your right. Soon your path leads down to a forestry track. Turn left along this and shortly cross two stiles to reach the road, near a footpath sign. Turn left and follow the road to a T-junction near Eel House. Those wishing to do the short walk turn left at this junction and follow the road until a footpath sign indicates 'Cunsey' to your left.

Longer variation. Cross the road and climb the stile ahead. Beyond this head up the field. After crossing the brow a stile will be seen ahead on the edge of a wood. Cross this and the wooden footbridge beyond to a T-junction of paths. Turn right and follow the path tunnelling steeply up and to the left through the trees. This path eventually emerges between gateposts and becomes more open. Soon it crosses a stream spilling down to the right, before climbing again to the left. In due course an old wall will be seen running alongside the path to your right. Eventually a gate, with a stile to its left, will be reached. Cross the stile and turn right to continue downhill, between deer fences, to a further stile and gate. Then go through a gateway in a wall. The path is well-defined now and continues to descend, generally bearing left, to pass through a gateway into a field. Continue down the field, with a wall to your right, to a gate to the left of a barn (High Dale Park). Go through this to meet a road and a footpath sign 'Eel House'. Turn left along the road, for about half a mile.

Just before reaching a house (Middle Dale Park), you will see a footpath sign to 'Cam Wood' directing you left. Follow this. The path leads to a gate and beyond this slants obviously uphill, bearing left. Eventually it climbs through a gateway, then between walls, then it forks. You bear left, between a wall and fence. The path continues upwards, bearing to the right through an area of young trees. There is, at the moment of writing, a fine view to the left across the wooded hills of the Grisedale Forest to the distant Coniston Fells. This section is somewhat moist underfoot! The ground becomes firmer when the highest point is reached. Eventually the path passes through an iron gate in a wall. Beyond this the path descends with glimpses of Windermere ahead, and the Fairfield and High Street fells rising distantly and beyond. The path finally emerges onto a tarmac road near a footpath sign 'Middle Dale Park'. Turn left along this road until you reach a footpath sign, pointing right to 'Cunsey'. You have now rejoined the shorter version of the walk.

Continuation for both short and long variations. Follow the 'Cunsey' sign. When the muddy track starts to swing to the right, away from the fence, look for a fainter path veering left towards the fence. Follow this. The path, muddy in places, keeps close to the fence. After passing an iron gate on your left continue with a firmer path which swings away into a wood consisting mainly of birch trees. Soon a ruined building is passed on your right. This is marked on the map as 'The Forge'. Beyond this the path forks. Keep to the right-hand fork which eventually bears left into the woods and then down to meet a tarmac road near Low Cunsey Farm. Turn right along the road. Look out for a 'Lake Shore Path' sign to your left, on a bend. Follow this. The next mile and a half gives delightful lakeside walking.

Unfortunately we are forced to leave the lakeside near 'The Bield' and go back onto the tarmac. Turn right along this road, bearing right at every junction, for the final mile of the walk.

Walk 7 **Medium Walk, 5 miles**

Gummer's How and St. Anthony's Chapel

A delightful walk packed with variety. It mixes superb views of Windermere and the distant high fells with sylvan woodland, delightful tarns and a fascinating sixteenth century chapel.

Parking: Leave Bowness by the A592 Newby Bridge road. When approximately seven miles from Bowness look out for a road branching abruptly uphill to the left, and back, signposted 'Kendal', on its left. If you find yourself in Newby Bridge you have missed it. Drive up this road until you see a 'Picnic Area' sign on your right. Park here (GR 389877).

GO BACK onto the road and walk uphill until you see a gate and sign 'Gummer's How' on your left. Go through the gate and follow the well-worn path, broken by occasional bands of steeper rock, up to the summit. From the cairn I'm told there is a good view southwards, across Morecambe Bay, and that given the right conditions Blackpool Tower can be picked out. I'm also told that from the edge nearest the lake there is a superlative view up virtually the full length of Windermere, with a backcloth, reading from left to right, of the Coniston, Langdale, Helvellyn and High Street groups of fells. I cannot verify this I'm afraid, for from this summit I've never seen anything but a few yards of wet mist. Return to the road by the same route.

Turn left up the road, go over the crest of the hill and turn right at the first turning. This side-road leads down to Sow How Farm. Go through the farmyard and follow the path across the field beyond to where a 'Public Bridleway' sign points left. Follow this. (The path continuing on beyond the sign is your return route). Soon the water of a tarn will be seen through the trees ahead. Pass through a gate and follow the path which goes to the right, around the tarn, crossing a footbridge over a beck. Just beyond this bridge climb up the bank to your left to reach the crest of the dam. Turn right and follow the edge of the tarn to a boathouse. From behind the boathouse follow a path through a gap in a wall and up towards a wood. This leads to a gate near a wall corner. Ignore this and follow a path to the right, with a wall to its left, to a second gate. To the right of this a second tarn will be glimpsed through the trees.

Go through this second gate and follow a path through the woods, curving to the right over boggy ground, to reach a tiny and delectably wooded tarn. The path goes along the dam and through bushes to meet a broader path. Turn left along this, passing to the right of a hut.

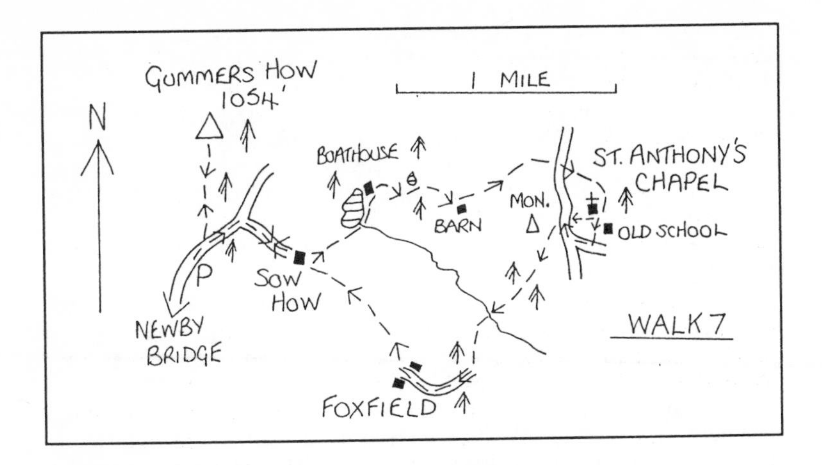

Go through a gate at the end of the wood into a field. Continue with a wall to your right to meet a path leading down to the right towards an old barn. Turn right down this to turn left at the barn and follow a path, with a wall to its left, which soon goes between walls to reach a gate. Go through this gate onto an open moor. The path bears first right and then left. As you proceed the view opens up across the Winster Valley. (The River Winster was once the boundary between Lancashire and the now defunct county of Westmorland. Westmorland, 'the land of the Westmoringas', a thousand years old name, was wiped off the map at the stroke of a pen by soulless bureaucrats).

The fell to your right, across the valley, is Whitbarrow Scar (Walk 16). The path goes down to a gate and beyond this twists more steeply down to a second gate leading onto a tarmac road. Across the road are two gates. Walk across and slightly up to the right-hand one. Beyond it walk to the right of a stretch of old wall and then downhill to pass between a barn and a ruin. Then bear right up a bank to see ahead a stone stile, of the type often called 'Fat Man's Agony', in the wall ahead. Squeeze through this and then bear left through two wall gaps before swinging right to reach the chapel of St. Anthony's of Cartmel Fell.

This is a fascinating sixteenth-century upland church built by the fellsmen in the sturdy no-nonsense manner they constructed their barns and farms. Built in 1504 it stands largely as the founders left it. Restored sixteenth-century stained glass, an enclosed pew that was perhaps also once a schoolroom, and a three-decker pulpit are the most obvious facets of its history. For a small donation a fascinating and more detailed pamphlet is available inside the chapel.

Leave the church by the lych-gate passing the old parish school. A polished rock outcrop opposite the school was the 'slide' of generations of schoolchildren. Soon you will come to a T-junction. Turn right and follow the road up the hill to a junction of roads at the crest. Look for a stone stile in the wall to your left signposted 'Foxfield, 1 mile'. This point can also be reached by turning right at the entrance to the church porch to reach stone steps in the corner of the churchyard leading up to another 'Fat Man's Agony'. Beyond this walk up through the trees to reach the road junction with the stile facing you. Above, on the crest of the hill, will be seen a column known as Rainsbarrow Old Man.

Cross the stile and follow a path uphill to reach another stone stile. Cross, and unless you wish to make the diversion up to the right to 'bag' the Old Man, continue with the path ahead to reach a further stone stile leading into a wood. Follow the path through the wood to reach a stile with an iron bar inset. Leave the wood by this stile and follow a path veering left. This joins a wider path. Turn right along this soon crossing a footbridge over a beck. This path goes through a gate into a walled lane. The lane climbs then swings left and soon the right wall veers away. Continue with the wall to your left to reach a white metal gate leading onto a tarmac road. Turn right along this. The road eventually leads between the buildings of Foxfield Farm. Bear to the right, in front of the farmhouse, and up a walled lane to a gate. Go through the gate and follow the path across fields and between rocky outcrops, ignoring all side paths, to meet your outward path at Sow How Farm.

STAVELEY

Walk 8 **Valley Walk, 5 or 6 miles**

The Upper Kentmere Valley

A delightful and amiable walk through a variety of scenery. Sylvan farmland gives way to rugged mountain terrain, a maze of old quarry workings and an artificially created, but nonetheless lovely, mountain tarn.

Parking: From Staveley follow the minor road signposted 'Kentmere 3½ miles'. When the village is reached follow the road up to and around the church. Park hereabouts. There are parking signs on the wall opposite the telephone kiosk (GR 456042).

LEAVE your car and continue up the tarmac road. At a junction continue straight ahead through a gate. I personally do not like road-walking and prefer to get it over with at the beginning of a walk; that is the reason why this walk is described as it is, for it would be equally interesting if reversed. The road winds around the foot of some crags with the valley gradually opening up ahead and giving glimpses of splendid scenery to take your mind off the hard tarmac under your soles. Ahead and to your left overlooking Kentmere Reservoir, are the steep craggy ramparts of Yoke, Ill Bell and Froswick (Walk 2). The head-wall of the valley is formed by the southern flanks of High Street and Mardale Ill Bell with the rocky dip of Nan Bield Pass to their right. From this pass the skyline rises to the rounded summit of Harter Fell, and the opposite wall of the valley is formed by the Harter Fell, Kentmere Pike, Shipman Knotts ridge (Walk 10).

Eventually the ways divide, with the tarmac road swinging away to the right and down to Hartrigg Farm in its protective wood. You now bear left up the rough road heading up the valley. This track eventually crosses a beck (Bryant's Gill) and passes below the steep rocks of Rainsbarrow Crag (look for climbers in action) to reach former quarry buildings surrounded by obvious evidence of their industry. Continue with the track past the buildings to reach the Kentmere Reservoir dam. If you are feeling energetic it is worth the extra effort to follow the path that encircles the reservoir. Although the ridge high above you is a very popular Lakeland fell-walk, the ridges and corries it throws down towards the reservoir and into the

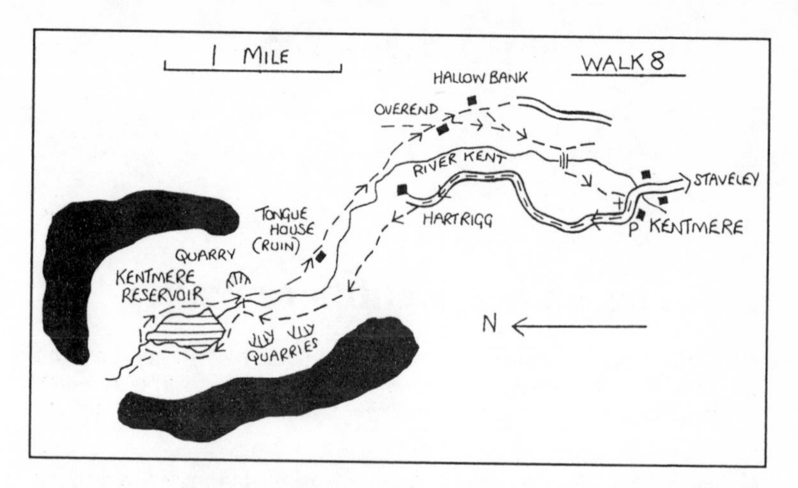

dalehead beyond its northern shores are rarely visited. By walking around the reservoir you obtain a real sense of remote and rugged fell country.

If however you prefer not to, simply walk across the dam to its far end. Here follow a path leading down behind the dam and through a gap in a wall. This path passes below an old sluice gate channel, then up and around to the right behind an old wall. It then follows this wall downhill before bearing away to the left to meet a further wall on its right. Continue with this wall on your right and ahead you will see spoil heaps. The path now nears the river, on your right, and follows it down to some grassy flats at the foot of the spoil heaps. (For those interested in old quarries all this area gives obvious opportunities for exploration. Be careful. Old quarry caves galleries are susceptible to rock-falls).

Continue past the foot of the spoil heaps to go down into a hollow between the fellside, on your left, and a spoil heap, on your right, to reach a wooden stile over a wall. Cross this and follow the path which bears left to reach a gate near a ruined building (Tongue House). Go left through the gate and then to the right, around the ruin. Almost immediately turn left, through a gap in a wall, and then right to follow a path running alongside a wall. This path is obvious having been used by wheeled vehicles. It continues across fields, gradually bearing left, to meet the river behind a screen of trees. These trees are interrupted by a fine packhorse bridge crossing the river with a gate to its left. Go through this gate and follow the path across a field towards a metal barn. Go to the left of the barn and continue with the track which now goes to the left of Overend Farm to make a junction with the path from Nan Bield Pass — notice the signs to your left. The track, a farm road now, continues past the front of the farm and uphill to meet iron gates across a concreted area with sheep pens to its left. Go through the gates and look for a 'Bridleway' sign on your right. Leave the tarmac road here and go down to your right, alongside a wall, to reach a gate, with 'Bridleway' on its far side. Go through the gate and straight ahead across a clapper-bridge over a beck and onto a path leading between walls. There are splendid views of the valley head, back to your right, from around here.

The walls soon veer away, but continue with the path, over a further clapper-bridge, into a walled lane. This lane is delightful to walk along. After passing through a gate the lane begins to climb; look for stone stiles in the walls to your right and left. Climb over the right-hand stile and follow the path down to a footbridge over the river. Cross the bridge and the field beyond to a gap in a wall leading into a walled lane. Turn left along this to pass through a gate to the left of a house and barn. Beyond this the lane divides. Take the left-hand branch which leads down to the tarmac road below and to the left of the church. Turn right to reach your car.

Walk 9 **Medium Walk, 4 or 8 miles**

Potter Tarn, Gurnal Dubhs and the Kent Valley

A walk offering a wide variety of scenery, ranging from two austerely lovely upland tarns to a delightful riverside. Nowhere excessively strenuous, all the climbing being done in the first third of the walk. Both short and long versions of the walk are equally worth doing, and it could be easily divided into two separate and entertaining walks.

Parking: The small car-park in Staveley, near the zebra crossing.

LEAVE the car-park, cross the zebra-crossing, and walk up the street signposted 'Kentmere 3½ miles'. Soon you will see a signpost on your left 'Burneside ▶'. Turn right, across the bridge over the river. Once over the bridge continue to follow the road bearing to the right, looking for a white house on your left named 'Riverside'. Turn left here and go between the houses to see a footpath sign 'Littlewood', on your right. Go through the gate ahead and up a field to a gate in a corner. Continue steeply uphill, keeping the wall to your left, to reach a stile in a corner. Beyond this continue climbing, with wall and fence to your left, the angle gradually easing, to pass through a gateway to the left of a wood. Head across the field, with wall away to your left, until a stile is reached in the wall ahead. Cross this and continue across the field beyond, following the line of an old wall, to find a stile in the wall ahead with a wall joining beyond it. Cross the

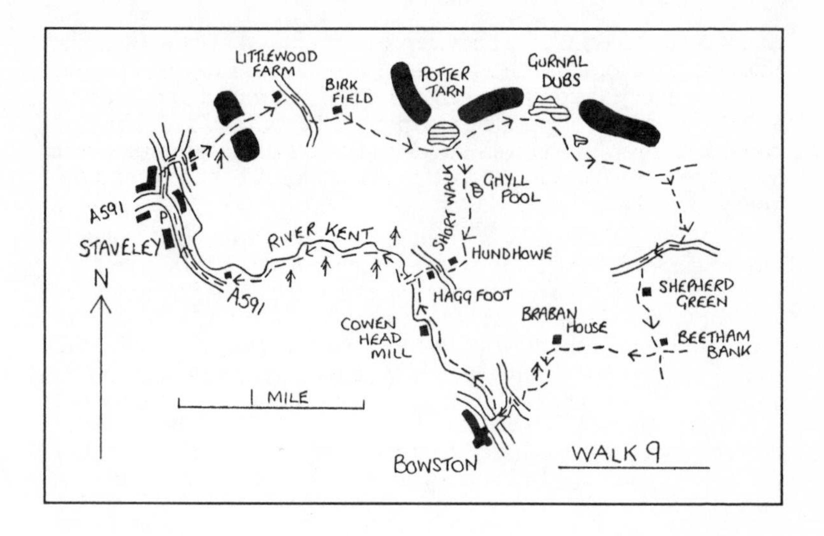

stile and go downhill, the wall to your left, to reach two gates. Go through the left-hand gate and keeping the wall to your right go down to Littlewood Farm. Go through a gate into the farmyard and beyond to a tarmac road.

Turn right along this road and follow it until a track is seen bearing away and down to the left, signposted 'Birk Field' above the wall corner to your right. Turn down this track to reach a gate. Pass through this and go down to a further gate marked 'Birk Field'. Beyond this pass in front of the house to reach and cross a stile to the right of a gate. Beyond this go between walls before turning right to follow the left bank of a beck. Eventually bear left away from the beck towards a gate. Go through this gate and uphill to a gate in a corner to the right of a tree and pointed rocks. This gate leads onto a wider track. Bear diagonally right across this track and follow a faint path climbing rightwards up the steep rocky fellside ahead to reach a gap in a wall. Go through the gap and shortly turn left through a gap in a higher wall. Climb up the fellside ahead to shortly reach the shore of Potter Tarn. Look back now for a distant but splendid view of the high fells. From left to right are Coniston Old Man, Wetherlam, Crinkle Crags, Scafell, Scafell Pike, Bowfell, Great End, Great Gable and the Langdale Pikes. A walk up the knoll to your right extends the view southwards towards Morecombe Bay and the Bowland Fells and more easterly the Howgills and distant Pennines. Continue alongside the tarn to find a stile over a crossing wall. Cross this and follow a path leading down and behind the dam.

Short walk. Those people wishing only to do the shorter version of this walk turn right at the foot of the dam and follow the path leading downhill with a little beck to its left. This leads through a gateway; below and to your left you will see the water of Ghyll Pool. The path continues down through gates, passing the pool, and continues down with Emanuel's Ghyll, the exit stream, to its left. The path eventually swings in towards the gill then follows a shelf running high above it. Soon a farm will be seen below (Low Hundhowe) and the mill at Cowen Head beyond it. The path bears left, passing to the right of a small pumping station surrounded by a metal fence, and slants down to a wall corner and two gates. Go through the right-hand gate into a narrow and somewhat overgrown lane. Follow this down, crossing a massive partially uprooted tree-trunk followed by a boggy section, to a gate. Go through the gate and pass to the right of an old but interesting-looking barn. Pass the end of the lane leading to the farmhouse and follow the lane leading down, right then left, to a tarmac road. Turn right along the road and shortly pass Hagg Foot Farm. Just beyond the farm a footpath sign (broken at the time of writing) indicates 'Bowston Bridge/Burneside' to your left. Go left then right through the farmyard and follow a path down, with a wall to its left, to a bridge over the River Kent and a junction with the longer route. Continue with this.

Long walk. Continue up and behind the dam to pass a notice prohibiting bathing, fishing, etc. Just beyond this and before crossing a footbridge over a stream look for a stile in the wall to your right. Cross this and go down and across a beck and follow a banked-up path to reach and cross a further beck. Bear right now along a faint path which soon swings left to climb uphill, below and to the right of a line of rocky outcrops. At the top of the hill a wall and stile are met. Cross the stile and follow a path down through heather to reach the shore of Gurnal Dubhs. Go to the right of this tarn, across the dam and along a well-defined path through the heather to meet a broader track and fence near a footpath indicator. Turn right along this path eventually to reach a gate. Go through the gate and follow the walled lane (Occupation Road) slanting across the face of the hill with a wide view to your right over the Kent Valley. Beyond this gate count the walls climbing up the fellside to your right. Just before the fourth one a red metal gate will be seen in the wall to your right. Go through this. Follow the wall down the field to go through a gateway into a second field. Continue down, with wall on your left, until just after passing a small walled enclosure, a path veers right and down to a gate leading onto a tarmac road, signposted 'Occupation Road'.

Turn right and follow the road until you see a walled lane leading left signposted 'Shepherds Green'. Turn down this into a farmyard and pass between the house and a caravan and climb into the green lane beyond. This climbs steeply, then bears right, before gradually descending to emerge onto a farm track just below and to the right of Beetham Bank Farm. Turn right down the track until it swings left across a beck and into a lane. You turn right here through a gate and keeping a wall to your left climb up the field. Pass through a gate in a fence and keeping the wall to your left continue to a gate in a corner. Go on to a further gate. Beyond this continue, with a wall now to your right, passing to the left of a wood. When the wall veers away head across the field to meet and follow a wall to your left. Continue into a boggy corner, just beyond a ruin, where a metal gate leads into a lane. Follow the lane to reach a farm road. Turn left and follow this road to a junction with a minor road. Turn right along this, shortly to turn left again towards the hamlet of Bowston.

Just before reaching the bridge over the river look for an opening on your right leading to metal gates. Turn down this to see a stile on your right just before the gates. Cross this and turn left to follow a fence around old mill ponds eventually to reach the river bank near a weir. Now follow the obvious path along the river bank, crossing stiles whenever they appear, to reach the mill at Cowen Head. Keeping the wall surrounding the mill to your left go through a gate and across a field to rejoin the river bank beyond the mill. Continue along the riverside path until a footbridge over the river is reached, and where the short and long version of the walk merge.

Cross the bridge and turn right to follow the river bank, passing through two gates below a barn. Continue with the riverside path which sometimes keeps to the water's edge and sometimes moves away from it and behind walls. Nearing Staveley the path moves away into a big field which narrows into a walled lane near where the river bends right. Continue with this lane which eventually moves away from the river and towards farm buildings. Go up through the farmyard to meet the A591. Turn right and walk through Staveley to your car.

KENDAL

Walk 10 **Fell Walk, 6-7 miles**

Harter Fell from Longsleddale

Longer and more varied than the John Bell's Banner walk but equally safe in that an accompanying wall or fence takes away all the problems of navigation for those who feel uneasy when the fells are wreathed in cloud. The walking is nowhere strenuous, the approach is interesting, and the views, particularly of Haweswater, are superb.

Parking: Take the A6 Kendal to Penrith road. Between four and five miles from Kendal look for a narrow road leading down into the valley on your left signposted 'Longsleddale 4 miles'. Follow this twisting road to its end, at Sadgill Bridge. Park near the bridge or on the grass verges of the old slate road ahead (GR 484057).

FOLLOW the slate road up the valley. The impressive crag rearing ahead is Buckbarrow Crag, with rock-climbs of varying degrees of difficulty on its steep, broken buttresses. Across the valley the rocks of Goat Scar offer a batch of short but fierce climbs. As Buckbarrow Crag is approached look for an access sign on your left. This leads to fine picnic and bathing sites on the bank of the River Sprint. An alternative to following the rough road is to scramble up alongside the cascades, pools and deep water-worn clefts to rejoin the slate road higher up, where it twists to the right around and above Buckbarrow Crag. The road ends at a gate.

Go through the gate to find a wall to your left, a steep path zig-zagging up the fellside ahead and a flattish boggy valley between grassy fells to your right. This boggy valley is the head of Mosedale, which leads down into Swindale. The fells guarding it are Branstee on the left and Tarn Crag on the right. Keep your eyes peeled around here for I have often seen deer at the head of Mosedale. The zig-zags ahead are your route to the crest of Gatesgarth Pass but before attacking them look for a stile over the wall to your left. Cross this and follow a path leading into the extensive but derelict Wren Gill Quarry. The diversion is worth the effort, especially to see one fine cascade which thunders down into a pit of piled blocks and disappears into some subterranean labyrinth to be regurgitated into daylight some considerable distance away. The earliest recorded reference to men quarrying Lakeland slate was in the time of Edward I, the

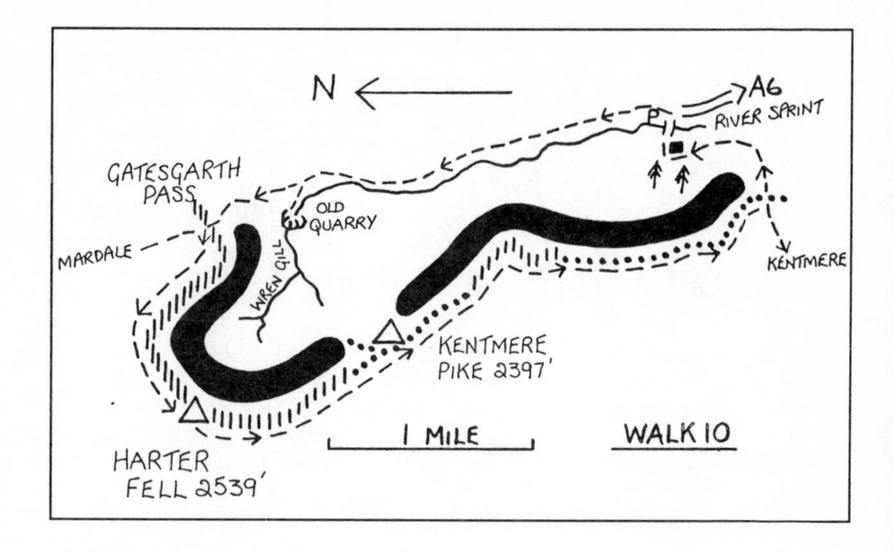

thirteenth century, and it is thought that the document refers to this site.

Having explored the quarry return to the zig-zags and climb up to reach the crest of Gatesgarth Pass, crowned by a fence and a gate. The path to Harter Fell is the well-worn one climbing up to your left and cutting a corner from fence to fence. Climb this until fence and path both veer up to the left. Move away to the right here to the edge of the fell for a bird's-eye view of Haweswater, long a reservoir for thirsty Mancunians. In a dry summer, delight in this view may be tinged with sadness at the sight of the walls and lanes leading down into the drowned valley and the blatant artificial beach encircling the lake. Return to the path/fence and climb up to the summit cairn.

This cairn, reinforced by piled remnants of the old iron boundary fence, looks like a stand of surrealist weaponry, especially when fronded with ice. The view is wide and comprehensive but particularly interesting is the detailed view of the rugged eastern flanks of High Street. A dark corner of Blea Water, once plumbed to a staggering depth of over two hundred feet, peers around the craggy flank of Mardale Ill Bell. For the descent continue with the fence, which veers southerly, eventually down into a boggy dip. The fence then gives way to a wall which climbs up to and over the summit of Kentmere Pike; the trig point is on the far side of the wall. Continue to follow the wall-fence-wall down the undulating ridge, with splendid views to the south and west. Kentmere is the valley to your right with the shapely trio of Yoke, Ill Bell and Froswick (Walk 2) forming its far wall. Keep to the crest for some fine aerial views down into the depths of Longsleddale. As height is lost the path on the right of the wall is the better one. Eventually wall and path drop down to a junction with the bridleway linking Kentmere and Longsleddale known unofficially to walkers, and some hardy cyclists, as 'Sadgill Pass'. This is yet another of Lakeland's network of old packhorse roads. Turn left and follow it down to Sadgill Farm and Sadgill Bridge.

Walk 11 **Medium Walk, 8-9 miles**

Keld, Swindale and Shap Abbey

This walk is a trifle boggy in patches and when mist shrouds the central section is no place for anyone who is not confident about their map and compass work. Given a clear day however it covers an obviously rarely visited corner of Lakeland and is full of interest. Red deer may be glimpsed and the bird life is varied. The scenery is a mixture of bleak Pennine and rugged Lakeland, whilst the 'Goggle Stone', Keld's tiny chapel, and the stark ruin of Shap Abbey will interest the historically minded. Despite its length it is nowhere particularly strenuous.

Parking: Take the A6 from Kendal. Upon entering Shap village, park in one of the lay-bys on the left-hand side of the main street.

WALK north along the main street to the fire station. Turn left here and almost immediately left again down West Close. Turn almost immediately right through a gate and follow a path up between walls and houses to the crest of a field. From here the distant fells above Haweswater may be seen ahead. Kidsty Pike is the obvious pointed peak with the dome of High Street to its left. Selside Pike, above Swindale, is to the left of High Street. The path goes down to a stile. Cross this and follow the path, alongside a wall, to a further stile. This leads into the field containing the 'Goggle Stone'. There are several similar monoliths scattered around Shap. An old drawing has revealed that once two impressive stone circles rose near the village.

Follow the path past the stone to a stile leading into a narrow lane. Cross the lane and climb the stile opposite into a field. Cross the field, passing the corner of a ruined wall, to reach a further stile. Cross this and head to where a footpath signpost rises above a wall. You will now find yourself at a junction of paths with the sign pointing back to 'Shap'. Ignore the stile leading onto the road and walk parallel with the road to another stile. Cross this and keeping parallel to the road go down the field to reach a stile leading onto it. Turn left down the road into the hamlet of Keld. The sixteenth-century chapel, now owned by the National Trust, will be seen on your left. A sign on the door informs you where the key is if you wish to see the interior. Go through Keld and follow the road beyond over a bridge across the River Lowther. Soon another bridge will be seen ahead. As you approach this look for a path crossing the beck to your left and heading up to the left of that bridge. Follow this path to reach a tarmac road. Turn left along this, first slightly uphill and then down to the right, to the second 'Passing Place' sign. Turn right here and follow a rough track leading up the right bank of Thornship Gill. This track ends above a small dam.

Across the gill, above the dam, are some rocky bluffs and on the skyline above these can be seen a barn with a wood to its right. Cross the stream and head up towards the barn. Looking back from here the distant dome of Crossfell, the monarch of the Pennines, can be seen beyond Shap village. There is no distinct path on this stretch and the ground is boggy in places. Just before reaching the barn and its protecting wall you will meet a sunken path running parallel to the wall. Turn right along this. Follow this, alongside the wall and climbing steadily, until you see a wooden stile crossing the wall. Turn right here.

You are now entering upon the boggy central section which could give difficulty in adverse conditions. After a few yards wooden stakes will be seen leading towards a hummock on the skyline crowned by a cairn. Head for this. From this cairn examine the skyline ahead. To your right is an obvious cairned hillock. Left of this is a dip and then the skyline begins to rise again. Head for the first obvious bump on this rise; the stakes will disappear before you reach it. Upon reaching it you will find a small cairn of weathered stones. Ahead now is a wide boggy hollow sloping down to the right. To your immediate left is a cairned hillock with a line of hillocks swinging right from this around the head of the hollow. Beyond these rise a line of higher and rockier summits with the cairned dome of Selside Pike rising above them. To the right of this fell is the obvious pointed summit of Kidsty Pike. Given you can see all this, head across the hollow in the direction of Kidsty Pike, ignoring Land Rover tracks that cross at right-angles to your heading. The beck you will cross is a feeder of Keld Gill. From the far rim look down into a further hollow with a wall running down to the right on its far side before turning abruptly away near a beck. Head for this wall corner. Near it a path will be seen crossing the beck and following its right bank. Follow this, soon the beck (Haskew Beck) drops into a wooded ravine (Gouthercrag Gill) and the path veers away to the right and drops between rocky outcrops before swinging left again towards the beck and steeply down into Swindale.

The steep crag across the beck is Gouther Crag, a venue for modern hard climbers. At the head of Swindale a path may be seen

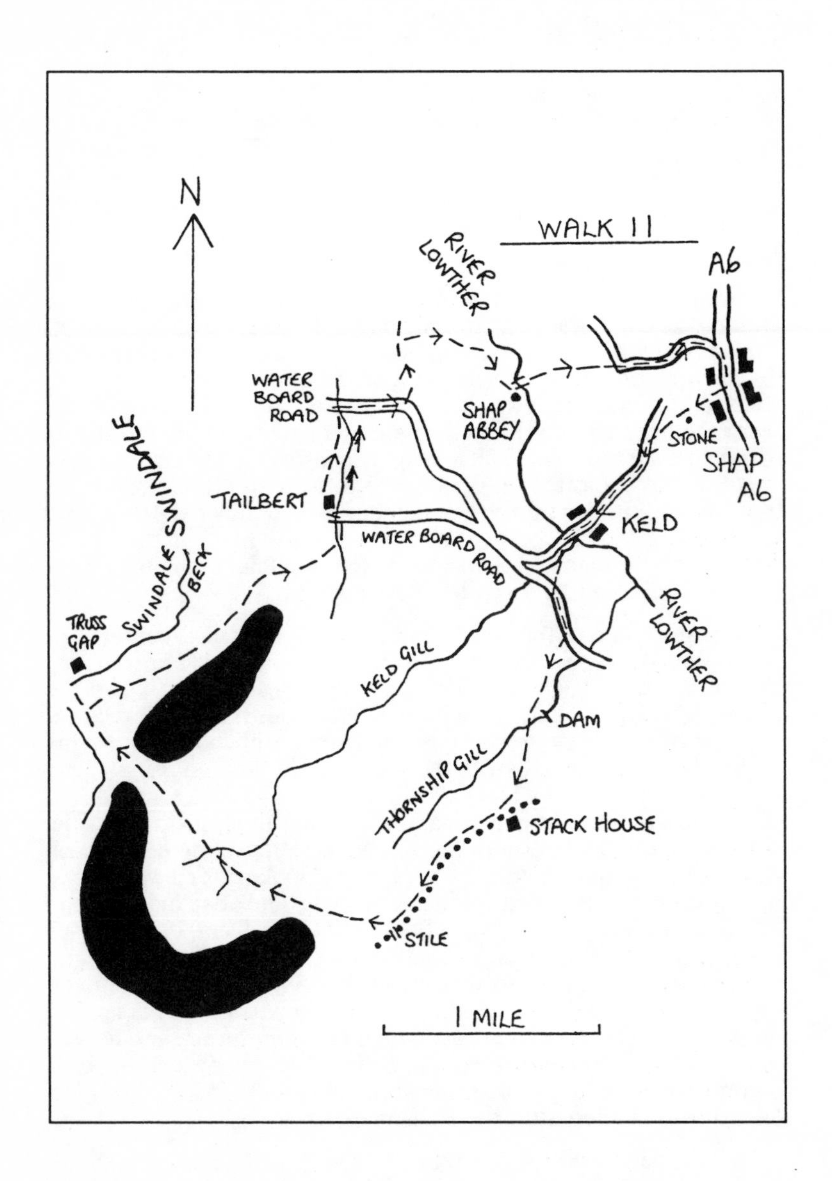

N
WALK 11
RIVER LOWTHER
A6
WATER BOARD ROAD
SHAP ABBEY
STONE
SHAP
A6
SWINDALE
TAILBERT
KELD
WATER BOARD ROAD
SWINDALE BECK
RIVER LOWTHER
TRUSS GAP
KELD GILL
DAM
THORNSHIP GILL
STACK HOUSE
STILE
1 MILE

slanting down the far side of the valley. This is the Old Corpse Road across which generations of Mardale dead were brought for burial in Shap, strapped to sleds or the backs of ponies. The farm below, across the river, is Truss Gap Farm, with stepping stones and a footbridge leading across the river towards it. Just before reaching the stepping stones turn right along a path that will be seen ahead climbing diagonally up the south wall of the valley. Follow this, ignoring a right fork soon after the start. The path skirts above a walled wooded enclosure and begins to steepen. Ignore a left-hand branch and a fine path bearing off to the right. Continue on, the path is faint here as it begins to swing to the right around the end of the ridge.

Soon a wall will be seen to your left with a ruined barn beyond. As you proceed another barn, overshadowed by trees, will be seen to its right. The path, becoming boggy, moves gradually nearer to the wall. When the wall swings abruptly left, near a beck, cross the beck then turn left to follow it down to a tarmac road. Turn left over a bridge over the beck and go through a gate and up behind the farmhouse (Tailbert). (For the next half mile we had difficulty relating the public right-of-way indicated on the map with the ground). Go through a gate on the left then turn right and follow a fence down the field, with a shallow ravine (Tailbert Gill) beyond it. When a gate in the fence is reached go through it and turn left to follow a faint path on the edge of the ravine leading down to a tarmac road.

Turn right along this and climb it to reach a track bearing left signposted 'Rayside'. Ahead the tower of the abbey will be seen rising out of the river valley bottom. Turn away from it and down the 'Rayside' track, looking for an iron gate on your right. (For the next quarter of a mile or so we again had some difficulty relating the right-of-way on the map with the ground). Go through the gate and cross the field to find a blocked stile in the wall ahead. Cross this to find a raised mound running parallel to the wall on its farther side. This is presumably one of the ancient 'dykes' drawn on the 2½-inch O.S. Map. Continue across the sloping field looking for a wall corner up to your right. Pass below this, crossing the line of an old wall, and head for the second telegraph pole below the wall corner. Continue beyond it to see a wooden stile in a corner below and to your right. Cross this and head towards the abbey, keeping well above the river, to reach a stile in a wall. Cross this and drop down to the track leading to the ruins. The abbey was founded in the 12th century and housed monks of the Premonstratension Order. The ruined bell tower is impressive; look for carved stonework in the wall of the nearby farm — probably looted after the Reformation.

Return back over the old abbey bridge (being replaced by a new bridge at the time of writing), and follow the concrete strip up to a cattle grid leading onto a tarmac road. This road joins the Bampton-Shap road. Follow the road back to Shap village.

The Whinfell Ridge and Borrowdale

An airy walk along a prominent ridge, followed by a leisurely return down a beautiful valley – the perfect recipe for a good day out. However, this is a trip that must be taken seriously. Carry a map and compass, and know how to use them; if the mist is down and swaddling the ridge, don't set out unless you're a sound navigator, and bear in mind that 11 miles over hill and dale is a long way, although there are several points along the route which allow you the option of a shorter walk.

Parking: Use the spacious, sign-posted parking area about 8 miles north of Kendal, on the A6 road to Shap. It's on your left as you approach from Kendal, just before the road goes over Borrow Beck via Huck's Bridge (G.R. 553037).

CROSS the road and walk back up it, towards Kendal, until you reach the end of a crash barrier. Turn behind the barrier and go down to and through a gate leading on to a rough track. Turn right, off the track, and climb directly up the steep flank of Ashtead Fell looming above. What path there is is faint and spasmodic and the going gets harder the higher you climb. Content yourself, however, with the comforting thought that there is nothing else as steep on the rest of the walk. This 'now-you-see-me-now-you-don't characteristic is a recurring feature of sporadic paths along the whole ridge, so don't rely on them too much. In this case, you can't go wrong if you simply keep making for the highest ground — the top's up there somewhere!

When you reach the top, you'll see a distinct cairn. To confuse you further, Ashstead Fell has three summits, of which this is the first. From here, take the path which follows the line of the ridge, tracing its way across the broad, rugged summit until you see a small cairn to the right: top number two. Now bear left along the path for top number three, which has a noticeable crown of rock on its head, and then drop down and continue until you meet a wall running across the ridge. If at this point you've had enough, go left along the wall and descend with it into Borrowdale, where a bridge carries a cart track across the beck. Stay on this side and follow the track back to the road.

To continue, cross the wall by an obvious broken section and begin the climb up Mabbin Crag, making always for the highest ground. The summit is marked by a small cairn, and from here you get a good view of the rest of the ridge: the first rise is Castle Fell, and then Whinfell Beacon; swinging left, the GPO radio station occupies a

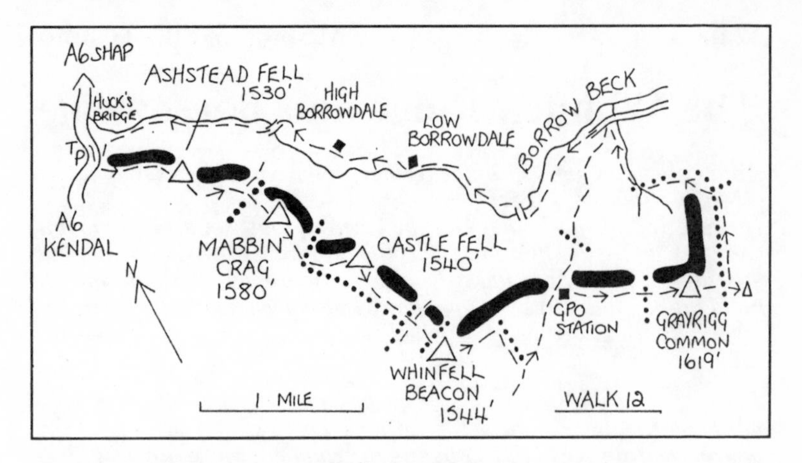

place below the slopes of Grayrigg Common.

Having seen what's to come, you can decide whether of not you want to go on. Should you pale at the thought, look ahead to where a wall crosses the ridge and meets another which follows the ridge ahead over Castle Fell. Make directly for the wall running across, and follow it left, back down to Borrowdale; then head up the valley to the aforementioned bridge and track, and follow the track back to the start.

If you're still with us, make for the corner of the two walls — a fence runs back from it, and about a hundred yards from the corner there's a stile; climb over, walk up to the corner and go through a gap in it, and then follow the wall uphill. As you reach the crest of the slope, there's a ring of old fence posts to your left, with the rounded summit of Castle Fell beyond them.

Having visited the summit, go back to the wall and resume your progress along its course, through one gate and then another where the wall turns a corner left. Once through the second gate, cross a track and head straight up the slopes of Whinfell.

A wall runs across the top of the fell, and can be crossed by either of two broken sections to reach the three large cairns which adorn the summit. The view from here is tremendous, particularly to the south-west, looking to Kendal and along the valley of the Kent out to the estuary, and beyond to the sea in Morecambe Bay.

From the cairns, walk in the direction of the GPO radio station — you should find a path which leads down the fell to an iron gate set in a wall. Go through, and follow a wide track down to a narrow tarmac road; turn left along it and walk up to the station.

When the road reaches the station gate, you have two choices. If you haven't the time or energy left to continue over Grayrigg

Common, descend left from the radio station and walk down to a gate in a wall; go through and follow a faint path down to the trees on the lower slopes of the fell; beyond the trees, the path will take you to the track in Borrowdale.

To continue, walk past the radio station, following the line of the ridge towards the rising bulk of Grayrigg Common until you meet a wall running across. Turn left along it, and just before it begins to descend, look out for protruding stones which make a stile to allow you over. Keep going towards the Common, with the ridge dipping a little before it meets the initially steep slopes of the fell. Slog your way up, and when the ground begins to level out you're onto the broad top. Now make for the Ordnance Survey column which marks the summit, at 1,619 feet the highest point on the ridge.

From here, looking east-south-east, the Howgill fells are gracefully impressive, with their ridges descending in sequence to the Lune Valley — walk towards them until you meet another wall crossing the ridge. Bear right along it to a wicket gate — you may not be able to open it, in which case climb over carefully — and make for a group of cairns notching the skyline at the end of the ridge, for a superb bird's-eye view down into the Lune Gorge.

Now make your way back to the wall and stay on this side of it, bearing right and following the wall's course down. The going is rough in places, with the ground dropping away steeply to your right into the Lune Valley.

Stay with the wall until you meet another crossing its path — where the two join there's a gap, which although partly blocked is passable. Go left, through the gap, and follow the other wall along the contour of the fell. Eventually, the wall crosses a beck running through a small ravine — ford the beck and climb over a ramshackle wire fence to the left bank of the ravine. You should find a path here, so follow it as best you can, taking always the same direction as the beck, until eventually you come to a bridge and a narrow road. Turn left along the road and walk back up the valley.

At the first gate, the road becomes a rough track; keep to it, through another gate and over a wooden bridge, to reach Low Borrowdale Farm. Go through a gate into the farmyard, and go across to another where the track takes up again, passing through a stand of trees to a gate. After the gate, the path forks — take the right fork up onto a grassy bank, and walk along the top until you meet a wall with yet another gate in it. Pass through and follow a track leading to the derelict High Borrowdale Farm. Keep the farm on your right and make for another gateway in a wall. Walk through and take the green track across the fields, easily traced over open pasture to a wooden bridge over Borrow Beck.

Cross the bridge and follow the track back to our starting point at the gate just off the A6.

A Circuit of Skeggles Water

A pleasant walk around a rather bleak upland tarn, followed by an interesting path along one of Lakeland's quieter valleys.

Parking: As for Walk 10.

CROSS Sadgill Bridge and turn left through an iron gate towards Sadgill Farm. There is a sign on the farm wall 'Bridle-path to Kentmere'. Go to the right of the farm, through an iron gate, and follow the stony track climbing up between walls to a further gate. Beyond this gate the right wall veers away. Continue alongside the left-hand wall to a further gate. Beyond this gate turn immediately left, walk past a stile over a wall, and cross a beck. Follow a path across the sloping field, with a wall to your left, and cross a insignificant beck to reach an iron gate in a wall.

Now follow an indistinct path which climbs diagonally up the field to the right, crossing a beck below a tree-filled cleft. Continue bearing right and uphill to reach a wall corner. Go through a gap in the right-hand (upper) wall and turning right climb uphill keeping this wall on your right. Eventually the wall gives way to a fence with an old quarry obvious beyond it. If in mist continue with this fence, which gives way to a wall again, to a junction with a descending wall. Turn left here and follow this wall down to a gate and stile. If the weather is clear, however, by simply keeping the fence/wall to your right the gate will be seen, with Skeggles Water to the left and below it. Head towards it, possibly finding a faint path.

Beyond the gate/stile the path is more defined and heads slightly left towards a ruin. Go to the left of the ruin, crossing a stream, to reach a gate in a wall. Beyond this the path goes through a boggy area to a further gate. Beyond this the path is more obvious and heads towards another ruin. Just before reaching this a path coming down from the right cuts at right angles across your path. Ignore this and continue on, going below and to the left of the ruin, between two trees. A boggy hollow is reached. Just beyond this turn left and follow a path leading towards a fence corner. This path continues to a gate near a junction of walls. Go through this and follow a well-defined path which soon begins to descend towards the lower Kentmere valley and distant Staveley. Look for a low ruin on your right and just beyond it a cairn to your left.

Here there is a junction of paths and this is where you commence the return leg of the walk. Turn left and follow a path which at first parallels the path you have just descended before swinging right towards a gate in a wall. Go through the gate to reach the bank of

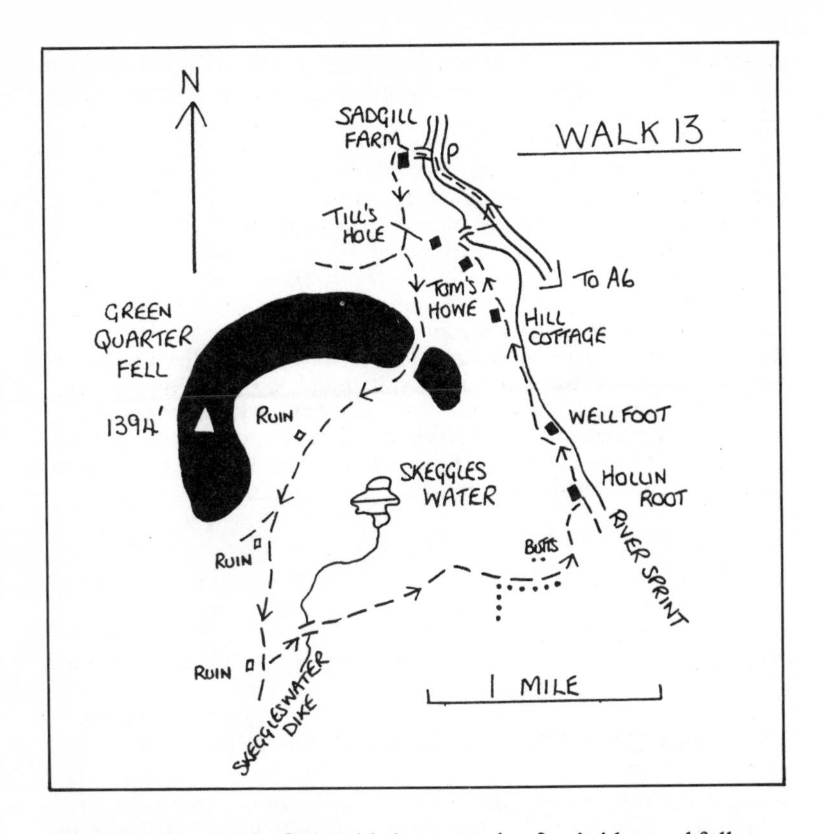

Skeggleswater Dike. Cross this by a wooden footbridge and follow a path to a gateway in a wall. From here look left, across Skeggles Water and into the head of Longsleddale, with Buckbarrow Crag's rugged skyline predominant. Beyond the gateway the path twists and turns across a featureless moor. When it appears to be approaching the rim of the valley look for a wall corner away to your right with a line of shooting butts to its left. When you can see a gate in a fence on the skyline ahead, with your path apparently heading towards it, leave this path and head towards the wall corner. Near the shooting butts you will pick up a good path which goes down to the left of a wall to meet a gate, in a corner of wall and fence.

Go through this and follow the path down, passing to the right of a ruin to a further gate. Beyond this follow the path bearing left and down through hawthorns. A gate is reached leading into a walled lane. Follow this down to a farm (Hollin Root). Go through a gate, then right through a metal gate. Then go left, around a building, to a further wooden gate. Beyond this follow a path, with a fence to its right, heading up the valley. This passes through a gate. Go through gate marked with a blue arrow, then immediately go through another gate to the left, also marked with a blue arrow, and keeping the farm (Wellfoot) on your right follow a path along the base of steep fields, alongside a fence. A gate in a corner, beyond a beck, is reached. Pass through this and continue along the river bank, passing a concrete bridge. Follow the cart-track leading away from the river and towards a gate, with a barn and a house beyond. Beyond the gate go through a gap between barn and wall and follow a fence around to a gate in a corner. Follow the path around the front of the house (Hill Cottage) and through a gate to reach a concrete farm road. Turn left along this. Just before reaching another farm (Tom's Howe), a gate will be seen on your right marked by a white footpath indicator. Go through this and down the field alongside a wall. Continue with now fence and river to your right to a gate. Go through this to a junction with the farm track to Till's Hole. Turn right here, across the bridge over the river, to reach the valley road. Turn left back to your car.

Walk 14 **Medium Walk, 6 miles**

Scout Scar and Cunswick Fell

Despite the walk's imposing title, it involves no strenuous ascents. Scout Scar and Cunswick Fell form a ridge, about 760 feet at its highest, between the Lyth Valley to the west and Kent valley to the east, a limestone escarpment presiding over good farmland and extensive woods more akin to the Silverdale area of North Lancashire than to anything in Lakeland. This is an easy walk on footpaths through fields and woods and along ancient, secretive lanes, enlivened by excellent views from the ridge.

Parking: From the centre of Kendal, turn up Allhallows Lane (signposted 'Hospital') opposite traffic lights and the Town Hall. Continue steeply uphill, following signs for Ulverston; after the road crosses a bridge over Kendal by-pass and begins to climb again, look for a car park sign just over the brow of the hill as you pass a prominent radio mast on the right (G.R. 488924).

LEAVING the car park, cross the road and turn right, downhill only a small distance to a footpath sign indicating 'Scout Scar' to your left. Go through the gate, ignore a path coming in from the left and take the obvious path ahead striking uphill, which eventually swings left to lead you along the top of the scar. The way now is easily followed,

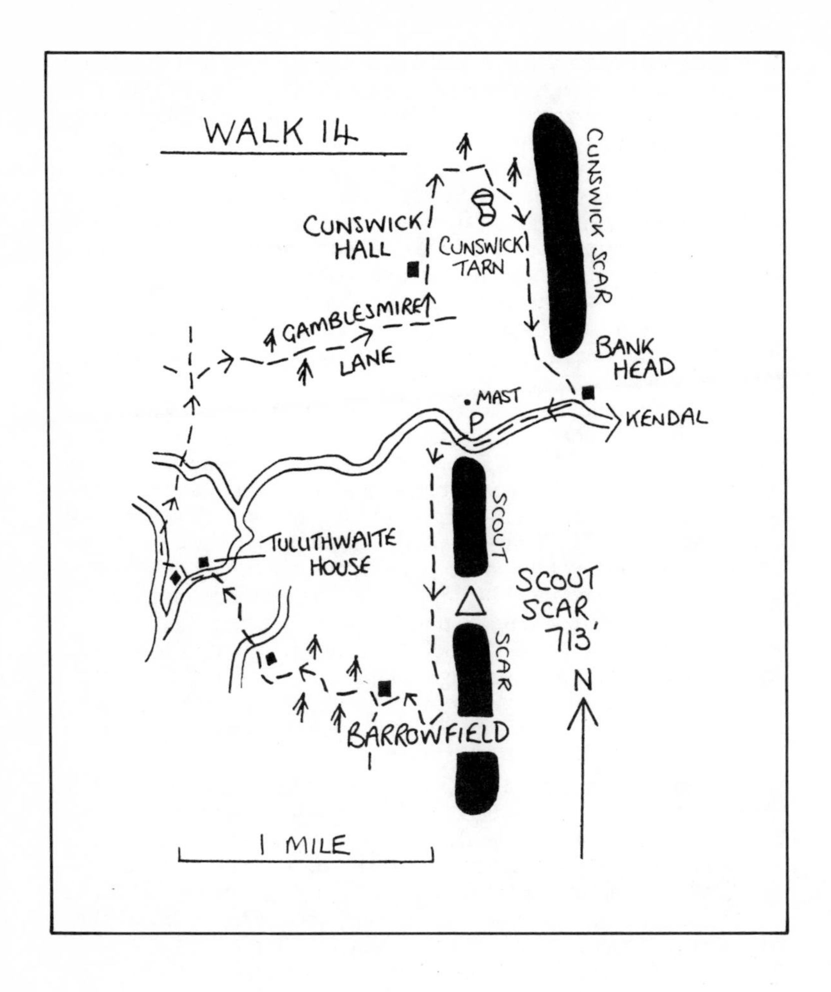

with the drop of the escarpment on your right. The path continues past a curious seat built of stone and roofed with a metal dome, and crosses a broken wall — if you wish to visit the triangulation point for a more extensive view, follow the wall up until the column appears on your right.

Returning to the path, continue as before until you reach a cairn on the right marking a path going off left — ignore this, but notice after a few more yards another, larger cairn, this time on the left. From here a path goes downhill to the right, coming soon to a fork — take the right fork, still descending, and follow it as it swings further right to lead through trees, eventually reaching the gate of a field. Enter the field, and follow a cart track heading towards a farm; on reaching it, notice a footpath sign on a gatepost directing you through the yard, then another on the wall straight ahead pointing left along a track; follow the track to a junction by a tree with path signs on it pointing right and left. Ignore these, and instead go into a rough, sloping field behind the tree and aim for its right-hand corner. Here you will find a small stile built into a wall; go through and follow a path through woods, descending to another stile at the woods' edge which allows you into a field.

To cross the field, bear slightly left, looking for another wall-stile at the far side — its location is just to the right of a big oak tree. Over the stile the path goes through a conifer plantation, coming soon to two junctions — at the first, continue straight ahead, and at the second soon after, take the well-defined path going left downhill. Still descending, the way bears gradually right and passes through a brackeny clearing, with wooden posts at intervals along the path. As the way goes into conifers again, keep a sharp eye open for a gap in the trees to your left, where the path branches to a field's gate. Ahead you will see a house; cross the field bearing left of it until you meet a wide, obvious track and turn right along it to reach a gate and stile; over the stile, follow the track to where it joins the drive leading from the house, and walk down it to a gate opening onto a very narrow road.

Turn left along the road and go through the first gate on the right, ignoring the rutted track ahead and bearing right towards a small field barn. A broad grassy track leads past the barn and brings you to a gate and wall with a stile in it; through this then go right to follow the field's edge round until you reach a metal gate; go through and bear left to a clapper bridge crossing a stream, then walk up the sloping field to a stile by a gate, which brings you out onto a road. Turn left, and follow the road a little way until you reach a house on the right called 'Rockfield' — turn up the drive, passing between the house and a garage, and make for the gate ahead; once through, go down to a stile; over this and then down to gate giving access onto another road.

Turn right along the road until you see a hedge-enclosed lane going off right, and walk along it until it meets a road — if you wish to shorten the walk, turn right to go back to the car park. To continue, cross the road and follow the lane on the other side, coming eventually to glasshouses and outbuildings and then a house — opposite on your right is a stile over a wall and wire fence. Climb the stile and walk up the field, with trees and a stream on your left, until you reach a gap in a broken wall; bear right now towards trees, soon meeting a well-defined farm track. From the track, head for a space between two trees where you will find another broken wall, then go left along the other side of it until you reach a stile. Crossing the stile, bear slightly right over this next field, seeing Scout Scar and the big mast near the car park directly ahead; on meeting a wall, turn right along it until you reach a gate. Go through and look across to the far corner of the field ahead, to a gate at the entrance of a lane running between hedges. Make for this, passing through another gate en route, and once there follow the lane first between dense hedging and then through woodland, until you reach yet another gate; pass through and follow the track uphill with the wall on your right.

To the left now is a splendid view of the Kent Valley and Kentmere fells, and a backward look reveals Wetherlam and the Coniston fells.

On reaching a gate at the end of the track, turn left and follow a track leading down to Cunswick Hall (a farm). Enter the farmyard, soon bearing right instead of going through the main complex of barns and byres, to take the farm's access road as far as a cattle grid — leave the road at this point and follow the wall on your right. Pass one plantation of trees and then reach another, where a gap in the wall gives access to a good path; follow it through the wood to another gap in a wall which brings you into a field where Cunswick Tarn can be seen ahead to the right. Looking left from the tarn, notice a gate in the corner of a fence, and walk over to it, then go through into the woods, taking a path going off right. On reaching a stile, climb over and take the path which leads left uphill; Continue steeply uphill, ignoring any path branching off right, until you are out of the trees and onto Cunswick Fell — look now for a kissing-gate in a fence on your left and go through it, turning right and keeping the fence on your right.

As you walk along the ridge, there are good views to the right of the Coniston Fells, Langdale Pikes and Red Screes, whilst to your left are the hills of Grayrigg Common and the Howgills above Lonsdale.

The fence soon becomes a limestone wall, which is followed until it turns a corner sharp right where a track issues from a gateway — take the track's left fork, downhill, and go past a bungalow and farm buildings on your left to a gate opening onto the road. Now point the driver to his right and send him up the road to the car park, waiting for him to pick you up on his way back!

Levens Park, the River Kent and the old Lancaster Canal

An easy but very rewarding walk, with a wealth of interest and varied scenery. It begins in elegant, landscaped parkland in the estate of Levens Hall, with its resident herd of deer, and from then on passes into wilder river country, up along the Kent, which hereabouts is in a lively mood through a series of small gorges, squeezed between rocks and crashing over falls in a frenzy of white water. The old canal is a strange delight – a waterless grassy trough with the towpath raised above it, passing in places through woodland where brambles and saplings have begun to colonize what was the canal bottom not so long ago.

Parking: About fifty yards north of Levens Bridge, on the grass verge of the northbound carriageway of the A6. Or go south over Levens Bridge and some distance beyond, to find a lay-by on your left (G.R. 496855 or 496848).

FROM the parking places, walk to Levens Bridge. Go into Levens Park by the public footpath sign on the north side of the bridge and follow an obvious track; it eventually fades but is still discernible, running through parkland with deer-fenced woods to your left.

The track becomes clearer again and then forks — take the left fork, leading to stone steps rising to a gap-stile in a wall. Go through and turn right, walking alongside the wall until it reaches a junction with another. Near the corner, a second set of steps takes you over the other wall.

From here, walk across the field towards a cluster of buildings and find a stile. Climb over to a narrow road and turn right, following the road to its end, where a bridge carries the A591 over the River Kent. Now descend some steps to a parapet leading under the bridge and emerging onto a minor road.

Follow the road, which runs parallel to the river, until you reach a junction and another bridge. Don't cross it, but go straight on and then take the first turning right. At a junction, keep straight on and follow the footpath sign for 'Wilson Place'.

As the road approaches a house, there's a suspension bridge on your right, over the river — go across and turn left along the river bank, following the path to a gate by a small wood. Go through, and continue until the path veers away right, between hedges; on your left, notice a gap in a wall and pass through, taking an obvious path on the river bank, crossing two low fence-stiles on your way and enjoying some classic river scenery, with the Kent dashing over its bed of huge tilted slabs.

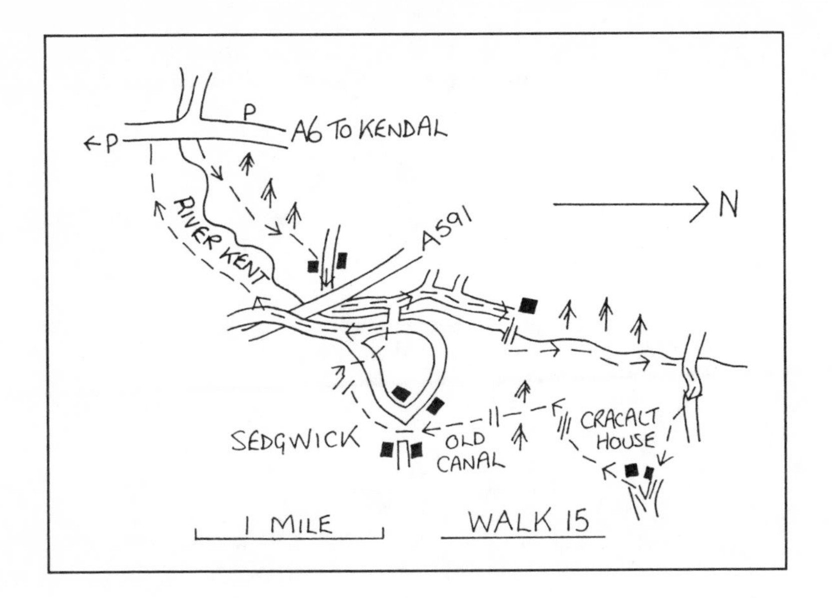

The path stays by the river, passing through two stone posts and then over a stone stile built into a wall. From there, follow the fence on your left around to a stile which lets you out onto a road. Turn right, and stay on the road until it takes a bridge across a filled-in section of the old Lancaster Canal. Walk over the bridge and then turn right onto a footpath signposted 'St. Marks Home', crossing the field to a gateway in a wall, through it and along a clear path to another gateway. From here, make for the farm ahead and enter the farmyard through a gate with an unusual fastening — you have to unscrew a nut and a bolt arrangement and put it back together once you're in!

Technical difficulties surmounted, cross the yard to a lane leading out and follow it to where another joins it, taking the sharp right turn along a lane flanked with iron fencing. It soon swings left in front of 'Cracalt House' and leads to a gate. Go through into a field and take a path running alongside hedging and a dry-stone wall, until it meets a farm access road coming down from the left — bear right and follow the road to a bridge over the disused canal.

Cross the bridge and immediately turn down the banking on your left, then through a gap-stile onto the canal towpath. Turn right, and follow the path to Sedgwick. At the first bridge you come to after the village, pass under through an iron gate and turn immediately right into an open field. Walk down the field towards a road, bearing slightly right to reach a footpath sign; go through the gate at the sign, cross the road and go through another gate, directly opposite, into another field. There's a faint path, but it leads straight to a water trough for livestock, so make a line to the right of it and cross the field to reach another road, where a gap-stile by a footpath sign lets you out.

Turn left, and follow the road to a bridge over the A591. Cross the bridge and look out for a drive-way on your right, which leads to a gate into Levens Park. There's a footpath sign indicating 'Levens Bridge', and a gap-stile right of the gate. Go through and bear left along a grassy, tree-lined avenue with a stream on your left. The way runs dead straight for some time then swings sharp right, following the river, as it approaches a wall. The track now leads, with the wall left and the river right, back to Levens Bridge on the A6, and the start of the walk.

Walk 16 **Medium Walk, 4½ miles**

Whitbarrow Scar

A delightful short walk giving extensive views over mountains and estuary. All the hard work is done in the first half hour, the rest is easy walking.

Parking: From Kendal take the A6 (Lancaster) road. Just before reaching Levens Bridge divert onto the A590 (Ulverston/Barrow) road. Four miles or so along this road look for a sign indicating 'Witherslack/Bowland Bridge' to your right. Follow this for about two miles, passing through the village of Witherslack, to reach Witherslack Hall. Park hereabouts on the grass verges (GR 438859).

FOLLOW the rough lane, signposted 'Whitbarrow', leading down to the right near the entrance to Witherslack Hall. At the foot of the lane go through a gate and follow a 'Footpath' sign, bearing left across a field. This leads alongside a football pitch to a gate in a wood. Beyond the gate obey the 'Footpath' sign and turn left. Continue with this path until a cairn is seen on your right and the path divides. Turn right here and begin to climb steeply uphill. The path gradually bears left and although steep is interesting, occasionally breaking out of the trees and giving views to the left over the Winster Valley towards Gummers How (Walk 7) and beyond. Eventually a gap in a wall is reached with a Nature Conservancy Sign. Go through the gap and

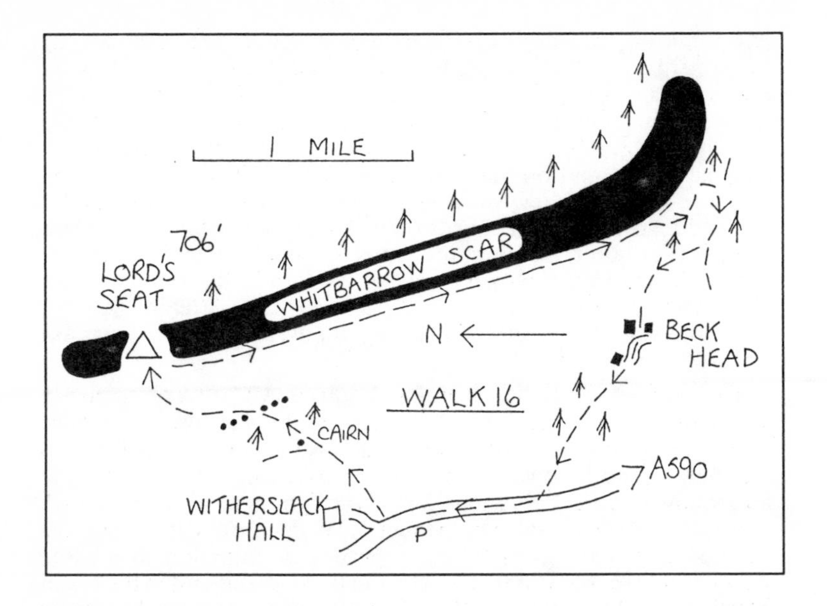

follow the path leading to the left. The angle is easier now and when the path forks take the right-hand fork. The ground becomes more open and the path is cairned. Look away to your right to see a fine pointed cairn on the skyline; this is Lord's Seat, the summit of the fell and your objective. When you can see this cairn look out for a path branching off towards it. This path starts just before a large cairn immediately to your right. Follow it to the skyline cairn and just beyond to a larger summit cairn incorporating a plaque dedicated to one Canon Hervey, a founder of the Lake District National Park.

The day I did this walk was one of the wildest and wettest in my experience. As I crouched behind the cairn bellowing details of the walk into my recorder over the scream of the wind, the sopping clouds flapped aside for a second of two enabling me to envisage that on a clear day the view to the north must be extensive, ranging from Coniston Old Man round to the Howgills. For the second leg of the walk turn south and follow the obvious path running along the broad crest of the ridge. Away to your left and parallel to the path is a long limestone 'scar' backed by woodland. Soon the path swings left to run below the scar. On a dry day some good fun could probably be had trying to girdle traverse the outcrop instead of walking along the path. A gap in a wall is passed and beyond it the path continues to a cairned grassy hump. Continue along the ridge over a succession of humps. Beyond the last obvious hump and as you approach the end of the escarpment the view over the Kent Estuary and Morecambe Bay begins to open up. The trees to your left now begin to veer away to the left, following the edge of the escarpment. Ignore the path heading towards them and follow the well-worn path bearing down to your right. This eventually passes the end of an old wall and swings to the left and down into trees. Eventually a gap in a wall is reached. Go through the gap but ignore the path leading straight ahead, which ends in a dead-end on the edge of the Scar. Instead, turn left and follow the wall for a few yards to another gap. Turn left through this gap and follow a path leading down to your right, away from a fence. Descend for about one hundred yards to where the path forks, just beyond a small cairn on your right at the foot of a prominent tree. Turn down the steeper right-hand path which is a little indistinct at first. (If you find yourself following a path over open scree you have just missed the turn-off).

The path soon becomes clearer and bears down leftwards to meet a churned-up and wider track. Turn right along this and almost immediately look for a path branching down to your left. Follow this fine built-up path down to a wider and level track. Turn right here and follow this track to a junction. Turn right here to follow a path signposted 'Beck Head'. This path gradually bears left and down to a stone stile. Cross this and follow the wall to your left to a white wooden gate in the corner of a field. Go through this and to the left of a building and greenhouse (Beck Head). Cross a drive and continue straight ahead, through trees, to a further gate leading onto a tarmac road. Turn right and follow this road to its end, then continue along a track past a house and barn. This bridleway leads pleasantly across the valley to a junction with a tarmac road. Turn right along this road to reach Witherslack Hall and your car.